WALKING IN CYPRUS

33 WALKS IN THE SOUTH, INCLUDING THE TROODOS MOUNTAINS

by Nike Werstroh and Jacint Mig

JUNIPER HOUSE, MURLEY MOSS,
OXENHOLME ROAD, KENDAL, CUMBRIA LA9 7RL
www.cicerone.co.uk

© Nike Werstroh and Jacint Mig 2025
Second edition 2025
ISBN: 978 1 78631 290 7
eISBN: 978 1 78765 246 0
First edition 2017

Printed by Bell & Bain, Glasgow, on responsibly sourced paper and other controlled sources.
A catalogue record for this book is available from the British Library.
All photographs are by the authors unless otherwise stated.

Cicerone's EU representative for GPSR compliance is Easy Access System Europe, Mustamäe tee 50, 10621 Tallinn, Estonia. Email gpsr.requests@easproject.com.

 Route mapping by Lovell Johns www.lovelljohns.com

Contains OpenStreetMap.org data © OpenStreetMap contributors, CC-BY-SA. NASA relief data courtesy of ESRI. Please be aware that the maps in this guide were created using open-source data and have not undergone the checking procedures of an official mapping agency.

In memory of Nike's grandma, who would have been proud to see this book

Updates to this Guide

While we strive to ensure that our guidebooks are as up to date and accurate as possible, changes can occur during the lifetime of an edition. Facilities, accommodation, transport and even rights of way can change, so if you find any inaccuracies in this book or have any feedback please let us know by email at updates@cicerone.co.uk. Updates will be published on the Cicerone website (www.cicerone.co.uk/1290/updates), so please check before planning your trip.

To receive free updates, special offers and GPX files where available, don't forget to **register your book** at the 'My Account' tab at www.cicerone.co.uk.

Front cover: View of the fire lookout station from the Madari Ridge (Walk 19)

CONTENTS

Map key 5
Route summary table 6

INTRODUCTION 9
Location and geography 11
Plants and flowers 12
Wildlife 13
Brief history 15
Religion 19
Getting there 20
Border crossings. 20
Getting around 21
Accommodation. 22
Tourist information 24
Language 24
When to go and what to take 24
Maps and waymarking 24
Using this guide 27

THE WEST AND THE AKAMAS PENINSULA 31
Walk 1   Aphrodite Trail, Akamas Peninsula. 33
Walk 2   Adonis Trail, Akamas Peninsula 37
Walk 3A   Smigies Nature Trail 40
Walk 3B   Pissouromoutti Nature Trail 43
Walk 4   Avakas Gorge 45
Walk 5   Petra tou Romiou Nature Trail 50
Walk 6   Horteri Nature Trail 53
Walk 7   Vouni path 56
Walk 8   Zalakas Trail 60

THE TROODOS AND CENTRAL CYPRUS 63
Walk 9   Marathasa Trail 65
Walk 10   Xystarouda – Agiasma – Vasiliki Nature Trail 68
Walk 11   Prodromos Dam – Stavroulia Trail 71
Walk 12   Kannoures Trail 74
Walk 13   Mnimata Piskopon Trail. 78
Walk 14   Atalante Trail 82
Walk 15   Artemis Trail 86

Walk 16	Caledonia circular	89
Walk 17	Pouziaris Trail	92
Walk 18	Loymata ton Aeton Trail	95
Walk 19	Madari Trail	97
Walk 20	Kannavia circular	102
Walk 21	Asinou Trail	108
Walk 22	Panagia tou Araka – Stavros tou Agiasmati	111
Walk 23	Politiko Nature Trail	115
Walk 24	Machairas Monastery – Fikardou	119
Walk 25	Kionia Nature Trail	123
Walk 26	Kakokefalos – Mantra tou Kampiou Trail	126
Walk 27	Dhyo Mouttes	129

SOUTH AND EAST 131

Walk 28	Hapotami Trail	133
Walk 29	Pissouri coast walk	136
Walk 30	Kyparissia Trail	140
Walk 31	Stavrovouni Monastery	143
Walk 32	Kavos Hill and sea caves	146
Walk 33	Agioi Anargyroi – Cyclops Cave	149

| **Appendix A** | Useful contacts | 153 |
| **Appendix B** | Further reading | 155 |

Acknowledgements

A big thank you to Jonathan Williams of Cicerone for giving us the opportunity to discover and collect Cyprus' trails all those years ago, and to everyone from the Cicerone team who worked on this book.

Map key

Symbols used on route maps

 route
 alternative route
 start point
 alt start point
 finish point
 start/finish point
 alt start/finish point
 woodland
 urban areas
 peak
 hotel
 hut
 campsite
 restaurant or café
 building
 church
 chapel/monastery/mosque
 water feature
 waterfall
· other feature
 viewpoint
 radio tower
ski lift
beach
picnic area
bridge
parking

Relief in metres

| 1800–2000 |
| 1600–1800 |
| 1400–1600 |
| 1200–1400 |
| 1000–1200 |
| 800–1000 |
| 600–800 |
| 400–600 |
| 200–400 |
| 0–200 |

Contour lines are drawn at 25m intervals and highlighted at 100m intervals.

SCALE: 1:40,000

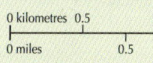

GPX files

GPX files for all routes can be downloaded free at www.cicerone.co.uk/1290/GPX

ROUTE SUMMARY TABLE

Walk	Start/finish	Total ascent/descent	Grade	Distance	Time	Page
THE WEST AND AKAMAS						
1	Bath of Aphrodite	380m	2	7.5km	2hr 30min – 3hr	33
2	Bath of Aphrodite	310m	1	7.5km	2hr 30min	37
3a	Smigies picnic site	180m	1	6.5km	2hr	40
3b	Smigies picnic site	140m	1	3km	1hr 15min	43
4	Near Toxeftra Beach	315m; via gorge: 200m	3	9km; via gorge: 6km	3hr – 3hr 30min	45
5	Aphrodite picnic site	135m	1	6.5km	1hr 30min – 2hr	50
6	Locality Platanouthkia	460m	1	5km	1hr 30min – 2hr	53
7	Pano Panagia	290m; via monastery: 335m	2	8.5km; via monastery: 10.5km	2hr 30min – 3hr; 3hr 40min	56
8	Trimiklini	260m	1	8.5km	2hr 30min	60
THE TROODOS AND CENTRAL						
9	Road junction near Pedoulas	700m	3	12.5km	4hr 30min	65
10	Xystarouda picnic site	660m	2	12km	5hr	68
11	Prodromos Dam picnic site	275m	1	9.5km	3hr	71
12	Near Agios Nikolaos tis Stegis church/Troodos Square	960m/115m	3	10km	3hr – 3hr 30min	74
13	Kampos tou Livadiou picnic site/Agios Nikolaos tis Stegis church	130m/960m	2	10km	3hr – 3hr 30min	78
14	Troodos Square	325m	2	14km	4hr – 4hr 30min	82
15	Troodos Square	215m; alt start: 170m	2; alt: 1	12km; alt start: 7km	3hr 40min; 2hr 30min	86

ROUTE SUMMARY TABLE

Walk	Start/finish	Total ascent/descent	Grade	Distance	Time	Page
16	Pano Platres	420m	2	9km	2hr 30min – 3hr	89
17	Pano Platres	430m	2	9km	3hr	92
18	Amiantos	150m	1	4km	1hr 30min	95
19	Locality Doxa Soi o Theos	690m; extension: 825m	3	13km; extension: 16.5km	5hr; extension: 6hr	97
20	Kannavia village	830m	3	19km	5hr 30min – 6hr	102
21	Agios Theodoros	375m	2	10km	4hr	108
22	Lagoudera	700m	2	15km	5hr	111
23	Near Machairas Monastery	330m	2	12km; circ: 8.5km	4h; circ: 2hr 30min	115
24	Machairas Monastery (or Kionia picnic site/Fikardou)	310m/280m; alt: 415m/745m	2	5km; alt: 10km	2hr; alt: 3hr 45min	119
25	Kionia picnic site	690m	3	15km	4hr	123
26	500m north of Kionia picnic site	790m	2	12.5km	4hr	126
27	1km south of Kionia picnic site	225m	1	4.5km	1hr 30min	129
SOUTH AND EAST						
28	Kato Archimandrita	290m	1	9.5km	2hr 30min – 3hr	133
29	Pissouri Beach	260m; with detour: 610m	2	8.5km; with detour: 12.5km	3hr; with detour: 4hr 30min	136
30	Germasogeia Dam	630m	2	12km	4hr	140
31	Stavrovouni Monastery	345m	1	5.5km	2hr	143
32	Cavo Greco Visitor Centre	150m	1	6.5km	2hr	146
33	Cavo Greco Visitor Centre	110m	1	6.5km	2hr	149

The narrowest section of the Avakas gorge (Walk 4)

INTRODUCTION

Aphrodite's birthplace, Petra tou Romiou

According to legend, the goddess of love and beauty, Aphrodite, was born in Cyprus. Her birthplace, Petra tou Romiou – the famous rock formation near Paphos/Baf – rising from the turquoise sea, attracts many tourists every day. Admiring the striking sea stack from the pebbly beach in the early hours before the coachloads of noisy tourists arrive, you can see why a goddess of beauty would rise from the sea on that very spot. Cyprus has a strong connection with Greek mythology, and today places of interest and even walking trails bear the names of mythological figures.

The scenery changes from the rugged coastline of the Akamas Peninsula, washed with turquoise water, to the wildflower-carpeted meadows and pine-covered slopes of Troodos; across the cultivated Mesaoria Plains to the narrow, serene Kyrenia mountains. The Kyrenia range leads to the Karpaz/Karpass Peninsula, which is like an outstretched arm pointing towards Turkey.

Sunshine, a Mediterranean climate and golden beaches with crystal-clear waters have attracted tourists for many years. But walkers – who prefer to leave the hustle of seaside towns, noisy taverns and the busy archaeological sites behind – have only just started to discover Cyprus' outstanding walking trails. The sound of waves crashing against the rocks and the smell of seawater accompany the walker on sunny coastal trails, while birdsong entertains them as they walk

Fantastic views from the Vouni path (Walk 7)

through the dramatic Avakas Gorge on the Akamas Peninsula. Hikers might spot shy mouflon (a type of wild sheep) hopping skilfully on the steep slopes in Paphos Forest.

In the centre of the island, in the Troodos mountains, zigzagging footpaths lead to small, hidden churches and Byzantine monasteries – many of which are on the UNESCO World Heritage List for their unique architecture and colourful frescos. Winding nature trails on pine-covered slopes with stunning views give walkers the opportunity to admire the beauty of these mountains.

Meanwhile, with castles proudly perched on rocks and mysterious monasteries in the shade of mighty trees, the thin, dramatic Kyrenia mountain range stretches across almost the entire length of Northern Cyprus.

In every season the island has its own magic to share with visitors. In some winters, snow covers the mountain peaks of Troodos, and Cyprus has Europe's most southerly ski resort. In spring, streams grow wider and colourful wildflowers carpet the meadows, while in the peak of summer the hazy air is filled with the chirping of cicadas. In autumn, families gather together to harvest grapes that grow on sunny slopes. At any time of the year elderly people are often found gossiping in front of their homes on the narrow streets of peaceful villages.

After a day spent exploring the trails, walkers might enjoy a well-deserved dinner in a rustic restaurant in one of the seaside towns or villages. Cypriot cuisine is strongly related to Greek and Turkish cuisine but with a local twist; fresh vegetables, olives, halloumi cheese, meat, fish and Greek yoghurt are among the ingredients common to traditional Cypriot food. Wine is a necessary accompaniment for local dishes, and in Cyprus people have been making it for thousands of years. Commandaria, the sweet dessert wine, is believed to be the oldest named wine in the world: it was served at the wedding of Richard the Lionheart in Limassol and the king was so impressed that he pronounced Commandaria 'the wine of kings and the king of wines'.

Due to its location, the island played a significant role in trading from around 3000BC and through the medieval centuries. It has belonged to different empires in its eventful past, with numerous artefacts and remains of ancient buildings around the island attesting to its diverse culture and troubled history. However, unlike other Mediterranean islands, it is not only the distant past that has left its legacy: after the island gained independence in 1960, tensions between the Greek and Turkish Cypriot communities grew, resulting in an eventual coup by the Greek Cypriots and an invasion by Turkey. The UN-controlled buffer zone (known as the 'Green Line') that runs like a long scar across the island, dividing its inhabitants, demonstrates that the recent past is still affecting the lives of many in Cyprus. This, as well as the island's earlier history, is described further in 'Brief history'.

While Cyprus may be politically divided, the amazing scenery can be enjoyed on the island regardless of political views. Cypriots – whether they speak Greek or Turkish, attend church or mosque – greet visitors with a friendly welcome. In this book we collected some of the best trails on the southern part of the island.

LOCATION AND GEOGRAPHY

Cyprus, surrounded by three continents, lies in the north eastern corner of the Mediterranean Sea. It is only 74km south of Turkey, about 100km from Syria and approximately 800km from mainland Greece. The island is 240km long and 100km wide at its widest point. It is the third largest island in the Mediterranean Sea, from which it rose millions of years ago.

The foundation rocks of Cyprus were once part of the oceanic crust of the Tethys Ocean and as such weren't connected to any continental plate. In the late Miocene period, the African Plate levered the floor of the Tethys Ocean, causing Cyprus to emerge. The Troodos mountains were once part of the ocean bed and today they form the best-preserved example of ocean floor on the Earth's surface. Here geologists can study the prehistoric sea floor.

Cyprus' two mountain ranges – the Troodos and the Kyrenia

WALKING IN CYPRUS

Violet bird's-nest orchid (Limodorum abortivum) in the Machairas forest

mountains – dominate its landscape. Troodos, located in the middle of the island, is mainly formed of igneous rock with its lower slopes covered by chalk. The Kyrenia, running across nearly the entire northern part of the island, consists of limestone and marble. About two million years ago the Kyrenia and Troodos mountains were islands; the land was constantly rising and the area between the two mountain ranges became the Mesaoria Plain.

PLANTS AND FLOWERS

There are approximately 1800 identified plant species on the island, of which around 140 are endemic. Some of the endemic plants' habitats are restricted to specific areas such as the Troodos mountains or the Akamas Peninsula.

Calabrian pine (*Pinus brutia*) forest, which thrives from sea level to an altitude of 1400m, covers the slopes of the Troodos and Kyrenia mountains and part of the Akamas Peninsula.

In Troodos the golden oak (*Quercus alnifolia*) appears at around 700m and the black pine (*Pinus nigra*) grows at higher altitudes. The Cyprus cedar (*Cedrus brevifolia*) can only be found in the Paphos Forest – especially around Trypilos Mountain. Cypress, juniper, alder and plane trees are quite common on the island.

The carob tree (*Ceratonia siliqua*) is typical to the Mediterranean region and has been used in many different ways since ancient times. It can be found growing in the wild but is widely cultivated for its edible pods. The word 'carat' – the unit used to measure the purity of gold – is derived from the Greek word *keration* as the pods' small seeds were used to measure gold in ancient times.

Colourful wildflowers begin to bloom from late February and the meadows can be carpeted with flowers well into May. Walking is the best way to observe the flowers, and even without specialist knowledge you can admire the extensive colours. Rock roses – their colours ranging from white and yellow to pink – often cover the hillsides.

There are more than 30 species of orchid that can be found in Cyprus, in places ranging from shady forest floors to rocky hillsides and the greatest number of wild orchids appear in March and April. The Cyprus bee orchid and the Lapithos bee orchid are endemic.

The island's national flower, the Cyprus cyclamen (*Cyclamen cyprium*), which blooms pink or white, flowers in the early autumn in moist forests. The dark-coloured, protected Cyprus tulip (*Tulipa cypria*) grows in the Akamas Peninsula, the Kormakitis Peninsula and in some parts of the Kyrenia range. The St Hilarion cabbage (*Brassica hilarionis*) can be found mainly in Northern Cyprus, especially near St Hilarion Castle.

Typical plants and flowers are labelled on most nature trails in Cyprus, so walkers can learn to recognise them.

WILDLIFE

There are 21 known species of mammal on the island. Only the luckiest walkers will spot the biggest of these – the shy Cypriot mouflon – hopping on the steep slopes in the less busy areas of the Paphos Forest and the mountains of Troodos. There is, however, a mouflon enclosure at Stavros Tis Psokas in Paphos Forest, providing an opportunity to see these endemic animals.

Mouflon once populated the mountains of Cyprus in greater numbers, but by the middle of the 20th

The whipsnake's bite is painful but non-venomous

13th-century Panagia Odigitria in Kouklia village

century hunting had decreased this population significantly. Then in 1939 the whole Paphos Forest was designated a Game Protected Area, and today it is also a Special Protected Area; thanks to these great efforts to protect the mouflon and their habitat, their numbers have increased to a satisfactory level.

Two bird species – the Cyprus warbler and Cyprus wheatear – are only found in Cyprus, and there is a conservation project in place to protect the endangered Griffon vulture.

Due to its geographic location, Cyprus is an important stopping place for migrating birds, and is therefore a great place for birdwatching. Unfortunately, despite the activity being outlawed in 1974, many birds are illegally trapped, killed and served as a delicacy in some restaurants.

Some of the sandy beaches on the island are important hatching places for the green turtle and the loggerhead turtle – both of which are endangered and protected. Turtles lay eggs every 2–5 years on the same beach where they were born, and development of the beaches means that the adult turtle might be unable to return to its birthplace. Tourism, fishing and pollution have decreased the number of suitable nesting beaches around the island, but there is now a great effort to protect the areas where the turtles lay their eggs. There are specially protected hatcheries at Lara Beach where visitors can learn about turtles and the effort to safeguard them.

A very small number of monk seals is believed to be living on Cyprus' remote shores. (It is estimated that there are fewer than 700 monk seals in the entire Mediterranean.)

Most of the snakes in Cyprus are harmless; however, the blunt-nosed viper is venomous but it only attacks in self-defence. Its body is about 1.5m long, silvery-beige in colour with rectangular markings and black spots on its head. It is usually found near water. If bitten by one of these, seek medical help immediately: call 112 or go to one of the hospitals or medical centres in the towns.

The 2m-long large whipsnake, which is shiny and black, is aggressive but non-venomous; however, its bite is painful so keep your distance.

Also common is the light-brown coin snake. There are dark coin-shaped patterns along its body and it can grow up to 1.7m. It might be aggressive but is non-venomous.

BRIEF HISTORY

Cyprus' eventful past, from ancient times right through the 20th century, could fill this book. This section gives only a very brief history, highlighting the key events which have shaped the Cyprus we see today.

The island has belonged to a number of different empires over the centuries, with each having an influence on its culture, architecture, cuisine and religion. This is very much in evidence on the walks, where you'll come across ruins, Byzantine churches, Venetian bridges, monasteries, castles and EOKA (National Organisation of Cypriot Fighters) hideouts.

Early history

There is evidence that Cyprus has been inhabited since 8000BC. Today, the ruins of city kingdoms in Kourion, Paphos, Soloi, Lapithos/Lapta and Salamis – each dating to different periods in the island's ancient history – are well visited by tourists.

The name 'Cyprus' means copper, and refers to the fact that copper was abundant here; however, it is unknown whether the island was named after the metal or the metal after the island. In earlier times the metallic copper was found on the surface. Copper was reduced to metal as pine resins in groundwater mixed with copper sulphate. Cyprus supplied the ancient world with weapons-grade copper, which was used to make swords and shields. When the copper was no longer to be found on the surface, Cypriots discovered that if cuprous earth and umber were mixed and then heated, they could get melted copper. Smelting began in 2760BC. Cyprus was an ideal place for mining and smelting as the island had all the necessary natural resources. The forests provided wood to fire the furnaces; they had to be replanted to meet demand, but the rainfall in the mountains made cultivation possible. Copper has been mined on Cyprus for 4000 years, producing millions of tons of slag. This used to be used to build roads but today the slag-heaps are protected monuments.

Cyprus was part of the Persian Empire and was only released from it in 333BC with Alexander the Great's victory over the Persian ruler Darius III. The island then became part of the Greek Empire. When Alexander died in 323BC, Cyprus was taken over by Egypt and became part of the Hellenistic Egypt under Ptolemy I, and the island's capital was moved from Salamis to Paphos.

In 58BC the Roman Empire annexed Cyprus and the following 600 years passed under Roman rule. There are many ruins of buildings and mosaics from this period which can still be seen today, such as the mosaics excavated at the Paphos Archaeological Site by the harbour of Kato Paphos.

Christianity appeared on the island in AD45 when Apostle Paul started spreading the new religion. The Church of Cyprus was set up by apostles and Cyprus became 'the Island of Saints'.

When the Roman Empire was divided in AD395, Cyprus came under the eastern half – the Byzantine Empire. During the Byzantine period (4th–12th century), many impressive churches were built and remarkable frescos were painted, such as at Agios Nikolaos tis Stegis (Walk 12), Asinou church (Walk 21) and Panagia tou Araka church (Walk 22).

The growing Islamic empire started to attack Byzantine lands in the 7th century; Cyprus, located between the two empires, was also attacked and many coastal settlements were destroyed in AD647. Castles and fortifications were built to protect the land from Arab attacks, and the ruins of St Hilarion, Buffavento and Kantara castles in the Kyrenia mountains are still visited by many.

The Middle Ages

On his third crusade, between 1189 and 1192, bad weather forced Richard the Lionheart's fleet to dock in Limassol. There, Isaak Komninos – emperor of Cyprus at the time – tried to capture King Richard's fiancée, Berengaria of Navarre, and his sister. In response, King Richard marched on Limassol and Komninos fled to Kantara Castle. In 1191 Richard married Berengaria in Limassol Castle, and Cyprus became the only foreign country where an English royal wedding was held.

Richard stayed in Cyprus for a year and during that time he conquered the entire island and then sold it to the Knights Templar. However, the Knights couldn't afford to keep the island and in turn sold it to Guy de Lusignan in 1192. From then until 1474 Cyprus was ruled by Lusignan descendants. Bellapais Abbey and many other splendid buildings were built during this period.

The last Lusignan king, James II, married a Venetian noblewoman who handed Cyprus over to Venice. The island was under Venetian rule

BRIEF HISTORY

from 1489 to 1571. Cyprus played an important role for the Venetians as a trading route and was used as a defence against the threatening Ottoman Empire. Forts were built around the big cities such as Famagusta and Nicosia/Lefkosia.

In 1570–71 Famagusta was attacked by the Ottomans and a year later the city fell. With this, a new era began in the island's history: Turkish settlers arrived on the island and for almost 300 years Cyprus was controlled by the Ottomans.

While the Ottomans left the Greek Orthodox churches intact, they converted some of the Gothic Catholic churches into mosques – for example, the Lala Mustafa Pasha mosque in Famagusta – and their influence on the culture and architecture of the island is still very much in evidence.

20th century

The origin of the campaign for *enosis* (union with Greece) can be traced back to the Greek War of Independence (1821–32) when the Greeks fought for their independence from the Ottoman Empire. Some Greek Cypriots also rebelled, but the Ottomans executed 486 Greek Cypriots – accused of conspiring with the Greeks – on 9 July 1821. The desire to become part of Greece grew stronger when Greece became independent in 1830, but Cyprus remained under Ottoman control until 1878, when it came under

The Kelefos bridge was built by the Venetians

The Kionia peak towers over the Machairas forest (Walk 27)

British control. The British assumed administrative responsibility while Turkey maintained sovereignty, then at the beginning of WW1 Great Britain annexed Cyprus and from 1925 the island was a Crown Colony.

The Greek Cypriots had hoped that British control would eventually help them achieve enosis. However, impatience grew and the Ethniki Organosi tou Kyprakou Agona (EOKA – National Organisation of Cypriot Fighters) was founded with the intention of ending British rule and achieving enosis. Between 1955 and 1958 EOKA carried out a series of attacks on the British military.

Turkish Cypriots only comprised a 17% minority of the population and they feared that if Cyprus achieved a union with Greece they would be excluded. Therefore they demanded *taksim* (partition), to divide the island between Greece and Turkey.

In 1960 Cyprus finally became independent, with Archbishop Makarios III becoming the first president of the Republic of Cyprus, but in 1963 serious violence broke out and the tensions between Greek and Turkish Cypriots increased. In 1964 a UN peacekeeping force arrived in Cyprus. Major General Peter Young drew a green line on the map, dividing the capital, Nicosia, between the Greek and Turkish. This later became known as the 'Green Line' and went on to divide the whole island.

In 1974 the Greek Cypriots, supported by the military junta in Greece, carried out a coup. In response, Turkey invaded the island. By 16 August 1974 the northern part – 37% of the island – was controlled by Turkey. The

190,000 Greek Cypriots that lived in the northern areas left their homes and lost their land and businesses as they fled to the south. Meanwhile, 50,000 Turkish Cypriots moved from the south to Northern Cyprus. A number of people were killed and many disappeared during the conflict, and the UN has controlled and patrolled the Green Line – which runs across the entire island – ever since.

In 1983 the Turkish Republic of Northern Cyprus – a self-declared state recognised only by Turkey – was announced. In 2003, for the first time in almost 30 years, the border was opened, allowing Cypriots to visit the opposing parts. Since then several border crossing points have been opened, allowing Cypriots and tourists to travel around the island.

Cyprus joined the European Union as a de facto divided island in 2004. The whole of Cyprus is EU territory and Turkish Cypriots are classed as EU citizens as they are citizens of the Republic of Cyprus (an EU country) despite the fact that they live in a part of Cyprus that is not under the Republic's government control. Since 2008 Southern Cyprus' currency has been the euro, while in Northern Cyprus it is the Turkish *lira*. Today, Nicosia is the last divided capital in Europe.

RELIGION

Most Greek Cypriots (who make up nearly 80% of the island's population) belong to the Orthodox Church of Cyprus, while most Turkish Cypriots are Sunni Muslims.

The Church of Cyprus is an autocephalous Greek Orthodox Church – meaning it has its own independent head bishop who does not report to any higher human authority. It is one of the oldest churches of this type. Ten of the churches built during the Byzantine period in the Troodos mountains are on the World Heritage List. Their steep-pitched wooden roofs are typical of the Troodos region, and some of the churches – for example, Agios Nikolaos tis Stegis near Kakopetria – also have a second timber roof. The UNESCO-listed Byzantine churches are also known for their frescos; some of them – such as Asinou church near Nikitari – have their entire interior covered in these paintings.

Monasteries were generally built in the mountains, so that the monks who lived in them could be further from temptation and closer to God. Many of these buildings also contain great collections of frescos. When visiting a monastery or church in Cyprus, wear long trousers and cover your arms. Some monasteries have a selection of robes by the entrance for visitors to cover themselves up with.

When Cyprus fell under the Ottoman Empire in 1571, Turkish settlers arrived onto the island and brought their religion, Islam, with them. During the Ottoman period some churches were converted

There are plenty of small waterfalls to enjoy on Walk 16

into mosques (for example, the Lala Mustafa Pasha Mosque in Famagusta), creating unique and impressive constructions. These – especially the ones in Nicosia and Famagusta – can be visited by tourists. You will have to leave your shoes by the door and women have to cover their head with a headscarf. Many well-visited mosques offer headscarves for female visitors.

Although the Turkish Cypriots in Northern Cyprus are Sunni Muslims, most of them don't follow their religion too strictly; they consume alcohol and women don't cover their heads in public.

GETTING THERE

There are plenty of direct flights from UK and many other European airports to Paphos and Larnaca/Larnaka in the south of the island. Shop around for the best deals. You could also check out the well-known tour operators; they offer package holidays, mainly for tourist resorts, but it's possible to book flights only with them. Easyjet, Ryanair, British Airways, Jet2 and Thomas Cook all have direct flights from UK airports.

BORDER CROSSINGS

The northern part of the island – the Turkish Republic of Northern Cyprus – is a self-declared state recognised only by Turkey. It is referred to as 'Northern Cyprus' by most outsiders, but the Greek Cypriots in the south consider it an occupied area. Since 2003 Cypriots from both sides have been allowed to visit the opposing parts, and tourists can easily visit both parts of the island.

The busy Ledra Street in Nicosia, lined with shops, cafés and restaurants, comes abruptly to the border crossing point. After presenting your passport to the two authorities you can continue on the very same street, but with a very different ambience. Many tourists visit both parts of the divided capital on the same day as EU passport holders don't need a visa to enter Northern Cyprus. There are several other checkpoints along the Green Line outside of Nicosia as well where you can cross.

Some car hire companies allow you to take a car hired in the south to the northern part of the island, but extra insurance will have to be purchased.

GETTING AROUND

Buses

If you want to get around by bus you need careful planning. There are buses running along the coast and serving some villages from Paphos, Limassol, Nicosia and Polis, but you need to check the timetables very carefully when planning a walk. Some villages are only served by one or two buses daily and a return journey can also be tricky. Check routes and timetables at the local bus stations and tourist offices before setting off for a walk.

Intercity buses connect major towns; for more information visit the town's bus terminal. You could also consult the local websites, but remember to check when they were last updated:

www.kapnosairportshuttle.com
www.intercity-buses.com
www.pafosbuses.com
www.cyprusbybus.com
www.limassolairportexpress.eu
www.limassolbuses.com

Bear in mind that many of the walks described in this guide start and/or finish in a remote place with no public transport, in which case a taxi or hired car may be the only option.

Taxis and car hire

While it may seem like a disadvantage to have a car parked at one end of a linear walk, most of the time it is possible to retrace your steps or arrange a pick-up service at the other end. This also applies if you're relying on buses, as you might get to the beginning of the linear route relatively easily but then need to call a taxi at the end of the walk. In the Troodos mountains you can find taxis in Platres and Troodos Square, and it is recommended to arrange the taxi before you start your walk.

Hiring a car is easy; cars can be booked in advance or are available in towns and are very reasonably priced. On Cyprus, drive on the left. Main roads are in good condition but you can easily find yourself driving on winding, single-lane roads with the threat of rock fall. Check with your car

Forested landscape above Agia Eirini (Walk 20)

hire company about any rules for driving on dirt roads.

If you hire a car in the south, you might be able to take it to the northern part of the island but you will need to purchase extra insurance.

Roads might be busy around the coastal towns and near the historical sights but many mountain roads are quiet. The driving habits in Cyprus may seem a bit more chaotic than in the UK, but locals know their roads and cars and they can recognise tourists on the road so driving is as safe as anywhere can ever be. A hire car is one of the best and easiest ways to get around the island.

ACCOMMODATION

Choice of accommodation is always a personal one, taking into account your budget and preferences. There are plenty of hotels and self-catering options to choose from in coastal areas, and there is a range of options in the Troodos.

As a walker you might opt to tackle several day trips in the same area, or you might consider splitting your holiday between different bases. If you decide to stay in one base, for example in a coastal town, you can still enjoy different areas on the island as many places are easily reached in a day trip. When choosing accommodation you might want to bear in mind that many towns have interesting sights that you can explore after your walk.

There are also some campsites on the island; a list of Cyprus Tourism Organisation (CTO) licensed campsites can be found at www.visitcyprus.com.

For accommodation resources, see Appendix A.

Dramatic coastal path near Pissouri (Walk 29)

TOURIST INFORMATION

The tourist information offices in Limassol, Polis, Platres, Paphos, Larnaca airport, and Agia Napa provide really useful information about trails and historical sites. Booklets about the most popular nature trails and the E4 long-distance trail (which was extended onto Cyprus in 2005) are also available from the Troodos Visitor Centre; some of them can be downloaded from the Department of Forests website: www.moa.gov.cy/moa/fd/fd.nsf (select the English-language option, if required, and then 'Informative Leaflets'). Check the opening times of the Troodos Visitor Centre as it varies.

It is best to ask for information about transport at the local bus terminals and Cyprus Tourism Organisation (CTO) offices.

You can also find useful information on the following websites:

www.visitcyprus.com
www.mytroodos.com
www.aboutcyprus.org.cy
www.choosecyprus.com

LANGUAGE

Greek and Turkish are the two official languages in Cyprus, and English is widely spoken. Signs are usually in Greek, and English is in use in the south; however, spelling with the Latin alphabet is not consistent. Names of places, villages, nature trails and historical sites are spelled in many different ways. See 'Using this guide' for details of the way in which place names are presented in this guide.

WHEN TO GO AND WHAT TO TAKE

Cyprus might seem like a year-round destination, but the best times for walking are the spring and autumn months. The summer months – from May to September – might be too hot for walking, although some of the trails in the cooler Troodos mountains might be considered. In autumn, although the land may be parched after the summer heat, there is scope for enjoying a much wider range of walks. Most rainfall occurs during winter, when snow can cover the Troodos. Perhaps the best time to discover the trails of Cyprus is the spring months, when wildflowers carpet the meadows and the temperature is warm but not too hot.

When preparing for a walk described in this book, pack what you would normally take for a day walk. Carry a waterproof jacket as showers can surprise you even in the spring. Take a jumper with you; Troodos is traditionally cooler than the coast. Comfortable hiking boots, sun cream and sun hat are all essential, and always carry ample water for your day.

MAPS AND WAYMARKING

Walking maps are not available for Cyprus. There are some tourist maps,

MAPS AND WAYMARKING

Clockwise from left: E4 Long Distance Trail sign; iron arrow in the Troodos; direction marker; many different direction markers used on nature trails

Map board

which you can pick up at the airports or in the tourist offices, but they don't outline the trails. You can also pick up leaflets of the popular nature trails from tourist information offices. You can use some of the well-known apps to find and record your walks, and for driving you will probably use Google navigation or similar.

The diverse trails in Cyprus range from rugged coastline to forest walks, a stroll between vineyards to walking in the mountains of Troodos. Nature trails are marked on the island, but these are not unified and many different signs are in use. At the beginning of the nature trails there is usually a map board with some information about the length and terrain and sometimes about the vegetation. Plants, flowers and trees are labelled along the trail so you can learn to recognise them. Benches are placed at some of the best viewpoints.

Some of the trails described in this book are based on nature trails. The Department of Forests has a booklet of the island's nature trails (see 'Tourist information', above), but some villages have created their own trails nearby and those are not listed by the CTO (Cyprus Tourism Organisation). Some of these routes start by the roadside and might end at a picnic site or another roadside; in such cases it is necessary to arrange a pick-up or plan to retrace your steps. These routes are usually not too long and walking back on the same path you may enjoy slightly different views. Paths used by walkers but not designated as nature trails often have occasional painted arrows and cairns.

The European Long Distance Path is marked with 'E4'. The E4 runs through Portugal, Spain, France, Switzerland, Germany, Austria, Hungary, Romania, Bulgaria, mainland Greece and Crete. The section in Cyprus was added in 2005 and it connects Paphos and Larnaca airports. It often follows tarmac roads but it aims to explore the diverse scenery of Cyprus. Some of the nature trails are part of the E4 and a few walks in this book follow some scenic sections of the E4.

USING THIS GUIDE

An information box at the start of each walk provides the following information: start/finish point (including GPS coordinates), length of walk in kilometres, amount of total ascent/descent in metres, difficulty rating (see grading information below), the length of time the walk is likely to take, and any details about refreshments and access that may be useful in planning. Note that where parking is mentioned it often refers to an informal parking area rather than an official car park. (At picnic sites there are usually plenty of places to park, and there are also often places for a couple of cars near the information board at the beginning of trails.) The relative difficulty of each walk (compared with the other walks in this book) is classified by grade.

Endemic Cyprus rock agama (Laudakia cypriaca)

Views towards the north from Madari Peak

The grading in this guide is only an indicator; bad weather, poor visibility and other factors can make any walk more challenging and even dangerous.

Grade 1: easy and/or short walk. Trail is without any significant ascent/descent. Waymarked route.

Grade 2: moderate, medium length or longer walk but mostly on easy terrain.

Grade 3: long walk and/or difficult terrain, or challenging route-finding.

The times provided – both for the walks themselves and between landmarks – are only an approximate indication. The walk times do not take account of longer breaks for picnics or visiting a monument, castle or church. The times given are fairly generous but it is always best to allow extra time. Once you have tried a few walks using this guide, you will be able to see how your own pace compares to the times given and adjust your planning accordingly.

The times and distances given in the route information boxes and route summary table are from the start to the finish of the walk. On there-and-back walks, the time is for the whole walk. On linear routes where the finish is different from the start, you will have to either arrange onward transport or retrace your steps to the start, in which case you would need to factor in additional walking time.

When planning a walk it is advisable to use Open Street Map (www.openstreetmap.org), Google Maps (www.maps.google.com) or a tourist map (available from tourist offices) to help locate the start point. Access to the beginning of the trails is described in as much detail as possible. To help identify the exact spot, GPS coordinates are also given.

Where there is water available on the route it is noted in the walk description, but you should never rely on it entirely as the tap or fountain might not be working at the picnic site when you get there. Occasionally there are warning signs – often only in Greek – that the water is non-potable (Μη Ποσιμο Νερο/ΜΗ ΠΟΣΙΜΟ ΝΕΡΟ). Always carry enough drinking water for your day.

Always try and check the visiting hours of churches given in this book as they can change from year to year.

In this guide, the spelling of place names in walk descriptions matches the spelling used on the maps in the guide, rather than what might be seen on signposts on the ground (which can vary along the trail). In addition, place names are given in both Greek and Turkish where both are in common use.

Places and features shown on the route maps are marked in **bold** in route descriptions to aid navigation.

The rushing Kryos river (Walk 16)

The term 'viewpoint' is often used to describe a place where you can get great views; this might simply be from a rock rather than a signposted viewpoint. Designated, marked viewpoints are noted as such in the route description. It was not possible to mention all the nature trails in Cyprus in this book and as you follow these selected trails you might come across other routes that you wish to explore.

GPX tracks

GPX tracks for the routes in this guidebook are available to download free at www.cicerone.co.uk/1290/GPX. A GPS device is an excellent aid to navigation, but you should also carry a map and compass and know how to use them. GPX files are provided in good faith, but in view of the profusion of formats and devices, neither the author nor the publisher accepts responsibility for their use.

A hidden peaceful viewpoint (Walk 20)

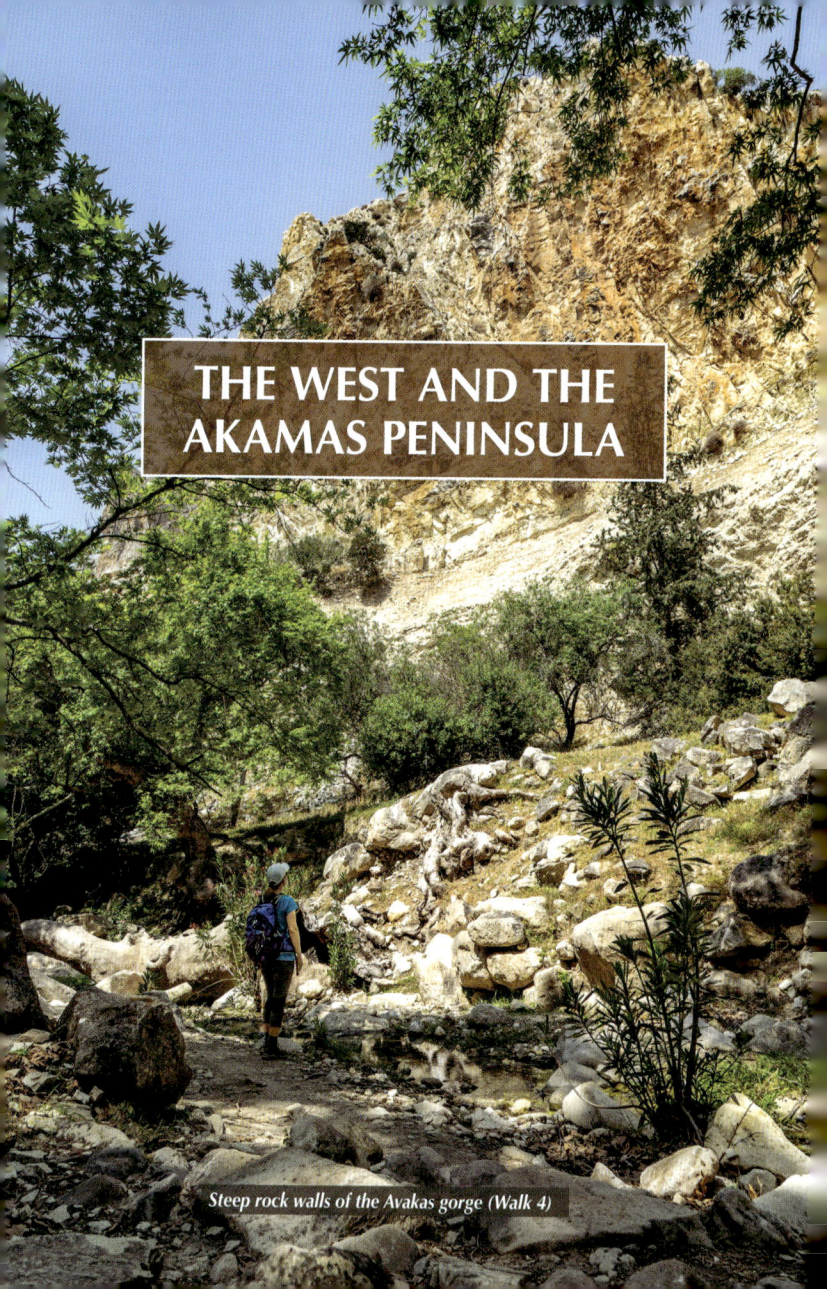

THE WEST AND THE AKAMAS PENINSULA

Steep rock walls of the Avakas gorge (Walk 4)

Coastal view from Moutti tis Sotiras (Walk 1)

The westernmost and least-inhabited part of the island, the Akamas Peninsula, is home to some of the best-known walking trails on Cyprus. Part of the Akamas Peninsula was once used by the British army as a firing range, but today it is a peaceful area for wildlife and for many of Cyprus' endemic plants. The rugged coastline is washed by turquoise water and it is not difficult to see why Aphrodite and her lover Adonis might have chosen to meet in this part of the island.

The area offers a variety of walks, from the dramatic Avakas Gorge to Paphos Forest where some of the intact medieval (Venetian) bridges can be found, as well as a walk between vineyards near Panagia village. Paphos is a great base for those who want to explore the trails in the west of the island. From self-catering accommodation to luxury hotels and resorts, tourists are spoiled for choice. For people who are fascinated by ancient history, there are plenty of ruins to discover. Paphos is known for its rich archaeological sites; the Paphos Archaeological Park, near the harbour, is famous for the mosaic floors of its Roman villas. The Tombs of the Kings – where aristocrats were buried in grand tombs carved out of rocks from around the 4th century BC – is a UNESCO World Heritage Site.

When the walking and sightseeing are over, there are plenty of restaurants at Paphos harbour where a range of Cypriot dishes can be enjoyed.

WALK 1
Aphrodite Trail, Akamas Peninsula

Start/finish	Bath of Aphrodite (N35.05610, E32.34589)
Distance	7.5km
Total ascent/descent	380m
Grade	2
Time	2hr 30min–3hr
Refreshments	Restaurant and bar at start point
Access	Road signs are easy to follow from Paphos and Polis. Regular buses from Polis. Parking available.

This is one of the most popular and well-known nature trails on the Akamas Peninsula. Coachloads of tourists visit the Bath of Aphrodite, but not all of them follow the goddess' footsteps all the way along this scenic circular trail. It is a moderately easy walk with gentle but stony uphill sections populated by juniper trees, with a steep descent giving excellent views to the Akamas Peninsula.

During the walk you can learn to recognise some of the plants of Cyprus, as many trees and flowers are labelled. The route is signposted with iron arrows and there are benches at the best viewpoints along the way.

There is a car park and a restaurant just outside of the Botanical Garden. Go through the gate – and then walk on the paved path which leads to the **Bath of Aphrodite**.

The **Bath of Aphrodite** is a small pool of water where a sign confirms that 'the Goddess of love and beauty used to bathe in the small pool of this natural grotto'. The pool area is usually very busy with people posing in front of the dripping water.

From the Bath, continue on the path marked 'Nature Trail'. When this paved path ends, exit through a gate then a few metres later turn left where a sign says 'Aphrodite and Adonis Trail'. The two trails run together for the first 2.5km, starting from the information board. According to legend, this trail was used by Aphrodite to walk back to her tower after bathing in the pool.

WALKING IN CYPRUS

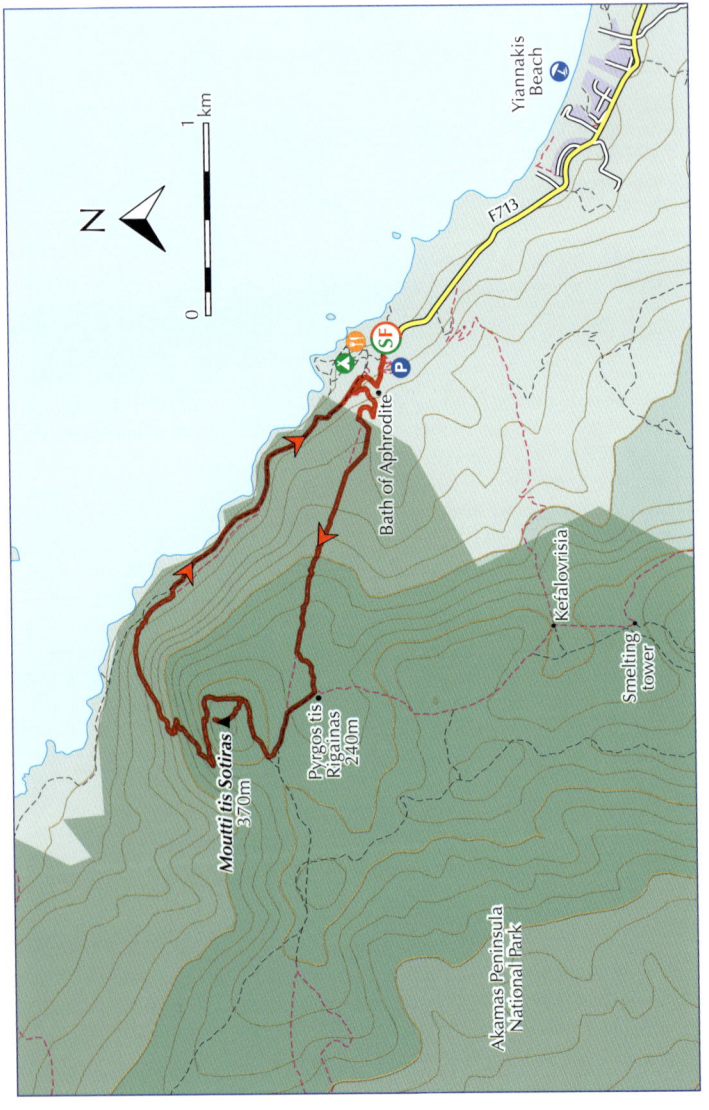

WALK 1 – APHRODITE TRAIL, AKAMAS PENINSULA

APHRODITE

There are two legends that link Aphrodite's name to Cyprus: her birth and the time spent with her lover, Adonis. According to legend, the goddess of love and beauty rose from the sea near Paphos after Cronos cut off Uranus' genitals and threw them into the water. Aphrodite was married to Hephaestus but had many lovers, the most famous of which was Adonis. Myrrha – who was to be Adonis' mother – was cursed by Aphrodite to fall in love with her own father, King Cinyras of Cyprus. When Cinryas found out that he'd been tricked, the pregnant Myrrha was banished. She changed into a myrrh tree and the baby was born from that tree. Aphrodite took baby Adonis to Persephone (goddess of the underworld), but she returned when Adonis was a grown, handsome man. Aphrodite and Persephone both wanted to keep Adonis. Zeus dictated that Adonis would spend one third of the year with Aphrodite, one third of the year with Persephone and could decide for himself with whom he would spend the rest of the year. He chose to spend it with Aphrodite.

Start walking slightly uphill on a stony path with occasional glimpses of the sea. Keep on the winding, well-trodden path, ignoring a narrow path on the right and noting the labelled trees and shrubs. As the path turns away from the sea the horizon fills with white limestones and pine-dotted hillsides.

Around the 1km mark the path levels out a bit and runs between thorny gorses. A few hundred metres later it crawls uphill again, and you find yourself walking on giant limestones before reaching a steeper section with some big stone steps. You are soon rewarded with views to the sea, and the path straightens again before climbing uphill for a short section after the 2km mark.

Ahead is the peak of Moutti tis Sotiras in the distance, but keep on the track gently turning away from the mountain. About 50min into the walk you arrive at a junction with a giant oak tree, a fountain and the ruins of **Pyrgos tis Rigainas** (Tower of the Queen). The trail divides here; the Aphrodite Trail continues to the right and the Adonis Trail to the left. Both are clearly marked.

Turn right on the Aphrodite Trail and follow the wide dirt road, occasionally marked with an 'E4', then turn right onto an iron arrow-marked path. Follow this marked path running parallel to a dirt road for a while. When you emerge at a wide dirt road, continue uphill with glimpses of the surrounding hills and sea. Look for the ruins of the tower down below.

At the end of the dirt road the path splits. To the left is a 5min walk to **Moutti tis Sotiras'** rocky peak, where a magnificent panorama of the Akamas Peninsula can be enjoyed. Take this, soak up the views and then retrace your steps to the junction with the iron arrow and continue to the left.

35

The path gives an excellent view of Chrysochou Bay

Soon the narrow path runs downhill with views to the sea and with towering rocks on the left. Iron arrows occasionally indicate the clearly visible path. Zigzag steeply downhill between wild thyme and thorny bushes for about 40min, and when you reach the dirt road turn right, towards 'Aphrodite Bath'. This road also has E4 signs.

Walk for about 20min on the dirt road with views to the rugged coastline and the hillside. Soon after you spot the caravans in the campsite, turn right where the sign shows 'Aphrodite Bath' and walk back to the pool and then to the **car park**.

WALK 2
Adonis Trail, Akamas Peninsula

Start/finish	Bath of Aphrodite (N35.05610, E32.34589)
Distance	7.5km
Total ascent/descent	310m
Grade	1
Time	2hr 30min
Refreshments	Restaurant and bar at start point
Access	Road signs are easy to follow from Paphos and Polis. Regular buses from Polis. Parking available.

The second best-known nature trail on the Akamas Peninsula runs along with the Aphrodite Trail for the first 2.5km – until the Pyrgos tis Rigainas.

A short section of the trail follows a forest track and then it runs on juniper- and pine-covered hillsides, dotted with white limestones with remarkable views to the surrounding hills and the sea around the peninsula. During the second part of the walk you pass striking rock walls in a dry streambed, and the descent at the end gives grand views to Chrysochou Bay. Spring is probably the best time to enjoy this trail, when the hillside is carpeted with colourful wildflowers.

From the car park, go through the gate and follow the paved path to the **Bath of Aphrodite**, where a sign confirms that 'the Goddess of love and beauty used to bathe in the small pool of this natural grotto'.

A path marked 'Nature Trail' continues from the pool. Shortly the paved path ends; exit through a gate and a few metres later keep left as the 'Aphrodite and Adonis Trail' sign indicates. (For the first 2.5km the two trails run together.) Follow the stony path uphill with occasional glimpses of the sea. Ignore a narrow path on the right and keep to the well-trodden path. Soon this bends away from the sea and the view is dominated by white limestones and pine-dotted hillsides.

The path levels out around the 1km mark, but a few hundred metres later it crawls uphill again and you walk on giant limestones before reaching a steeper section with steps. There are some views to the sea and the path first levels out and then climbs uphill for a while after the 2km mark. Ahead in the distance is the peak of Moutti tis Sotiras, but the path bends away from it and about 50min after starting the walk you arrive at a junction with a giant oak tree, a fountain and the ruins of **Pyrgos tis Rigainas** (Tower of the Queen). The trail splits here; the Adonis Trail continues to the left and Aphrodite Trail to the right.

ADONIS

Adonis – the god of beauty and desire – was born to Myrrha and King Cinyras of Cyprus. Aphrodite and Persephone both wanted to have him, and when Zeus announced that he could spend one third of the year with Aphrodite, the second third with Persephone and he could choose who to spend the rest of the year with, he chose Aphrodite. Adonis died after being attacked by a wild boar, believed to have been sent by one of the jealous gods. He died in Aphrodite's arms and anemones grow where his blood is said to have fallen.

The forest track leading to Kefalovrisia

Take the path on the left, marked 'Adonis Nature Trail' and 'E4'. The well-trodden path gently crawls uphill between bushes and juniper trees. About 20min later it crosses an overgrown track and shortly joins a forest track with a green arrow. A few metres later an E4 sign can be spotted, marking the direction of the Adonis Trail. Follow the forest track downhill and leave it to the left where the green arrow and a battered E4 sign indicate. Approximately 1hr 20min into the walk you'll arrive at the forest junction of **Kefalovrisia**.

Turn left on the path marked 'Adonis Trail'. Walk alongside a dry streambed with rocks towering above on the left; in front, like a

WALK 2 – ADONIS TRAIL, AKAMAS PENINSULA

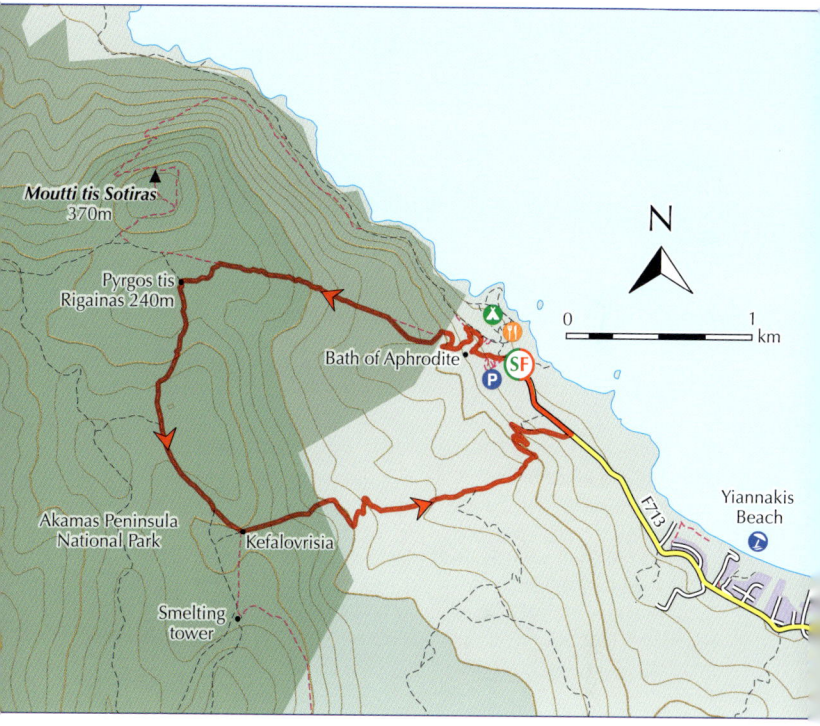

well-designed postcard, a green meadow stretches out with the blue sea in the background. The rough path, with a water pipe in the middle, runs steeply downhill and when it becomes smoother you can enjoy the views without the worry of tripping over stones. Occasional green arrows and E4 signs mark the way.

The path widens and levels out, and soon the Adonis Trail leaves the wide track to the right. (There is no arrow to mark this fork, but a little green nature trail label keeps you on the right path.) You soon reach a viewpoint, from where you go steeply downhill. Ignore two consecutive dirt roads joining from the left. Shortly after the second of these, leave the track slightly to the left on the bend as the green arrow indicates. Before long there is another steep descent and you can spot the car park and restaurant near the Bath of Aphrodite, where the walk began. The path runs alongside a fence before it reaches the road; turn left on the tarmac road and walk back to the **car park**, which is 5–10min away.

WALK 3A
Smigies Nature Trail

Start/finish	Smigies picnic site (N35.02352, E32.33367)
Distance	6.5km
Total ascent/descent	180m
Grade	1
Time	2hr
Refreshments	None
Access	Follow the Elia Tavrou road into and through Neo Chorio village. The tarmac road turns into dirt track and leads to Smigies picnic site, where there is space to park.

Two nature trails – which could easily be tackled one after another – start from the popular Smigies picnic site. As on many nature trails, plants and flowers are labelled along the way, but the waymarks are not always consistent.

This route follows a footpath which occasionally meets and runs along a dirt road for a while. In the spring, rock roses and wildflowers colour the hillside of Pissouromoutti. It might not be a challenging walk but remarkable views welcome you on Pissouromoutti. Most of the walk is exposed without much shade.

Start at the Smigies picnic site by the information board showing a map of the circular walk and take the stony path that winds uphill behind the board. The landscape is dominated by Pissouromoutti's rocky top on the left. There is no shade on the hillside and it can get very hot on a sunny day.

About 15min after leaving the picnic site you arrive at a viewpoint, from where there is a clear view towards the sea. (If you observe the rugged coastline carefully, you may spot some sea coves.) On the right at the top of the rocky hill is the Piana fire lookout station building. Continue on the path and soon reach a dirt road; keep left, as the green arrow indicates, and follow this slightly downhill (the right fork goes up to the **fire lookout station**).

Continue on the track – lined with pines and with sea views on the left – to the next intersection, where you follow the nature trail sign straight on. Soon you arrive at another intersection, where the path on the right-hand side is the short version of the nature trail and returns to Smigies picnic site. Follow the 'Long

WALK 3A – SMIGIES NATURE TRAIL

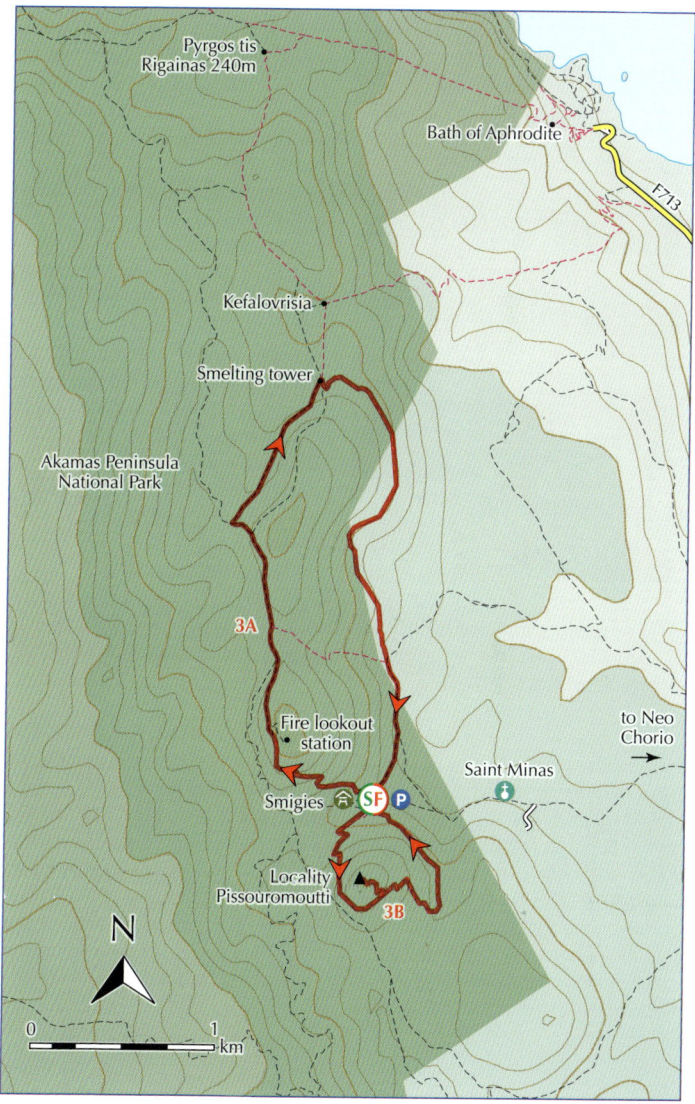

Smelting tower by the former magnesium mine

Way 5km' sign on the wider track, straight on. Here the path runs on level ground with excellent views. Ignore the adjoining dirt road on the right and keep straight on as the track bends slightly left. Very soon, at the next junction, go right as the green arrow indicates.

Follow the dirt track slightly downhill by the dry streambed. Juniper and pine trees are the main vegetation on both sides of the road. Pass the ruins of a house and then go downhill. After the 3km mark, follow the green arrow to the left. Approximately an hour after leaving Smigies picnic site, notice the **smelting tower** of a former magnesium mine on your right. Walk up to the tower and a little further on you will find the shafts of the mine.

A number of **magnesium mines** in the Akamas region were abandoned at the beginning of the 20th century. Today the remains of kilns indicate the former mining activity.

Standing with the kiln and entrance holes on your right, continue straight on and slightly downhill, on a narrow path between bushes. Soon spot the green arrow sign. The stony path runs along the rock rose-covered hillside with views to Chrysochou Bay. The fire lookout station comes back into view and you descend gently. Keep on the small path, ignoring other paths crossing your way. This becomes smoother and runs beneath pine trees before descending on the rocky hillside.

When the path meets a dirt road, keep straight on. (The small path joining in from the right is the other end of the 'short way' that peeled off from the nature trail after the fire lookout station.) When the dirt road splits, follow the one on the right and walk back to the **Smigies picnic site**.

WALK 3B
Pissouromoutti Nature Trail

Start/finish	Smigies picnic site (N35.02352, E32.33367)
Distance	3km
Total ascent/descent	140m
Grade	1
Time	1hr 15min
Refreshments	None
Access	Follow the Elia Tavrou road into and through Neo Chorio village. The tarmac road turns into dirt track and leads to Smigies picnic site.
Note	For map see Walk 3A

At the opposite end of the Smigies picnic site there is another information board with a map of the short Pissouromoutti Trail. The circular route starts gently uphill just behind this board.

From the Pissouromoutti information board, start on the path winding gently uphill on the right. The path follows the contour of the hillside and just after the 0.5km mark it bends away from the fire lookout station, with excellent views to the sea on the right.

Locality Pissouromoutti

A small chapel hidden among carob trees

About 30min later you'll reach a junction with a 'Pissouromoutti View Point' sign. From here it is possible to follow the narrow, grassy path running amid rocks and overgrown by wildflowers, to the top. The path might be difficult to spot. On the peak of Pissouromoutti (**Locality Pissouromoutti**) (400m) a fantastic 360-degree panorama greets you.

From the peak, retrace your steps to the junction with the viewpoint sign and continue downhill to the left. This section is easy to follow as it descends gently on a grassy path. A few minutes later, join a track overgrown by grass; keep right and follow it for about 50m.

Leave the track to the left on a narrow path, marked with a good-sized arrow made of stones on the grass. This pleasant path descends through lush vegetation to a forest road, which is only 5–10min away from the stone arrow. Turn left onto this and a few metres later take the path on the left. It first runs parallel to the forest road, then gradually leaves it behind and returns to **Smigies picnic site**.

WALK 4
Avakas Gorge

Start/finish	Car park 900m E of Toxeftra Beach (N34.92048, E32.33796)
Distance	9km; return via gorge: 6km
Total ascent/descent	315m; return via gorge: 200m
Grade	3
Time	3hr–3hr 30min
Refreshments	Viklari restaurant near the gorge; restaurants at Agios Georgios and Lara Beach; water at car park
Access	From Agios Georgios on the F706 road, head north towards Lara, follow to Viklary 'The Last Castle' car park and turn right towards Avakas Gorge. It is a dirt road but in fairly good condition; in dry weather most cars can take it without any problem.

The first half of this walk involves a scramble through huge, impressive rocks in a narrow gorge. Following the Avgas river, you hop from rock to rock in the water surrounded by massive rock walls for about 3km. Most people only walk up to the narrowest part of the gorge, so the further you get the fewer people you are likely to encounter. At the end of the gorge you can either retrace your steps or return to the car park via a dirt track.

As the gorge is very narrow near its start, the water level can rise rapidly after heavy rain and create a flash flood. It might not be possible to pass the narrow section if the water level is high. During heavy rain or thunderstorms walkers should avoid the gorge.

In addition, rocks can be slippery and the ground is loose in many places. There is a risk of rockfall and grazing goats could knock down rocks from above at any time.

About 900m from Toxeftra Beach there is a designated car park with a picnic area, information board and toilets. The stony path starts by the information board and then runs between juniper trees and soon arrives at another information board.

About 800m from the car park you enter the gorge. There is a towering limestone wall on your right as you walk on the narrow but well-trodden path by the

WALKING IN CYPRUS

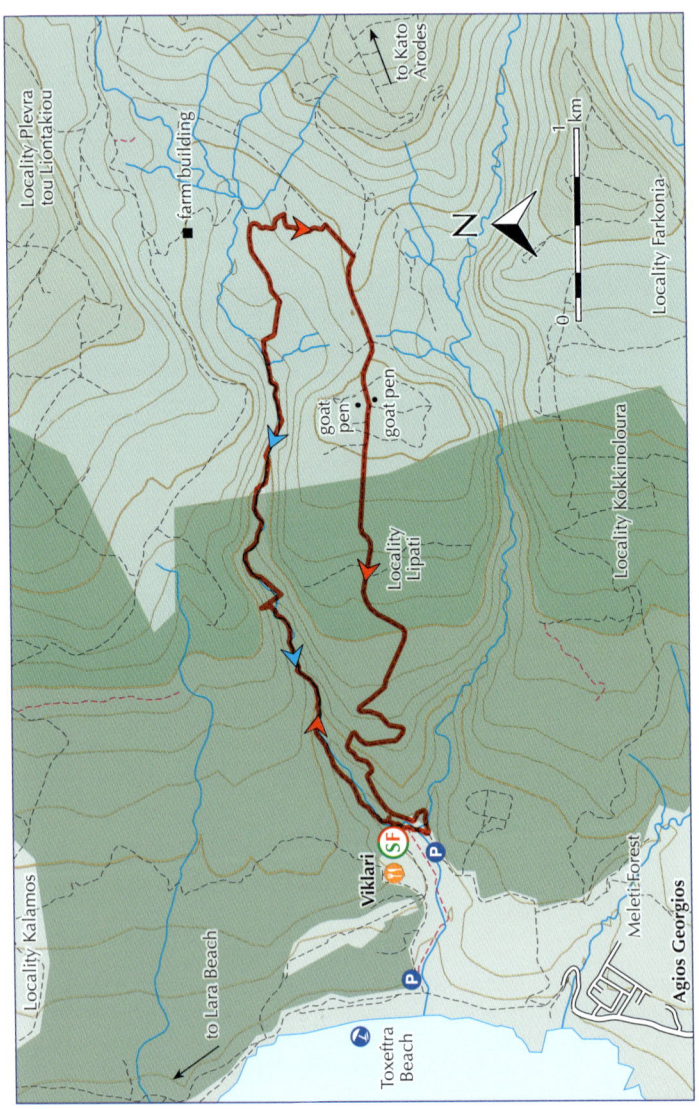

WALK 4 – AVAKAS GORGE

stream. Cross the stream on rocks several times before reaching the narrowest part of the gorge.

> The **Avakas Gorge** was formed by and named after the Avgas river. The name Avgas originates from the Greek word for egg, and it refers to the fact that many birds – including the endemic Cyprus wheatear and Cyprus warbler – live and nest in the gorge.
> Water has eroded the limestone rocks, creating an impressive narrow gorge.

Enormous rocks cast shade into the thin pass; birds swoop and settle on their nests built into the sheer rock face. Look up to see the huge rock stuck between the edges of the gorge above you. From here, you scramble and climb through many boulders of various sizes and cross the stream numerous times before reaching the end of the gorge.

Soon after its narrowest section the gorge widens up a bit, with bushes and trees clinging to the rock walls and the banks of the stream becoming denser. At times it might be difficult to see the path, but stay close to the stream, which you cross several times on rocks as you progress.

The ground might be loose here, so extra care should be taken. You may have to deviate from the 'main' path depending on the water level and vegetation on the banks as well as rockfalls.

Most people only walk up to the narrowest section of the gorge

Some light scrambling over boulders

WALK 4 – AVAKAS GORGE

Notice a big plane tree with its roots clinging to the loose soil on the left. Climb up to the ledge and arrive at a clearing with wildflowers and with limestone cliffs on the left. A few minutes later you are back to the streambed; continue between boulders and rocks.

You'll see a rusty old trailer crushed on rocks to the left-hand side and a few minutes later you'll spot the other part of the trailer in the water, partially buried under the sediment. Soon another riverbed joins from the right, but carry straight on to reach a narrow section overgrown with reeds. There is a 'path' on the ledge on the left or you can go through the reeds. Shortly afterwards, climb the steps out of the gorge onto a grassy clearing.

> The nearby green and white **hills** are dotted with goats and sheep. Grassy lands scattered with white chalk and limestone patches dominate the surrounding hills.

There are two options here: you can either return the way you came or take a circular route back to the start.

Return via the gorge

If you enjoyed scrambling through boulders in the gorge you might want to go back the same way – but allow at least the same amount of time for returning as it took to reach this point.

Circular return

If you want to get back to the car park a bit quicker, or if it is not safe to return through the gorge due to rain or the threat of rain, there is an option to follow a dirt track for about 5.5km, and it will take just over an hour to get back to the car park.

Emerge from the gorge to the grassy clearing, by a bench and warning signs. Keep right and shortly after reach two isolated shrubs with two benches. Go left on a track and less than 10min later when the track splits, keep right. Shortly after meet another track by a map board, go right and at the next junction bear right again on a chalky track.

About 15min after reaching the white chalky track you pass some ramshackle **goat pens** with sheep and goats nearby. As you descend between juniper trees, enjoy spectacular views to the shore, Lara Beach and then Agios Georgios by the sea. At the junction go right and shortly arrive back at the **car park**.

WALKING IN CYPRUS

WALK 5
Petra tou Romiou Nature Trail

Start/finish	Aphrodite picnic site (N34.674871, E32.606047)
Distance	6.5km
Total ascent/descent	135m
Grade	1
Time	1hr 30min–2hr
Refreshments	Souvenir shop with refreshments at the beach car park
Access	Petra tou Romiou picnic site is located along the B6 road about 2.5km from Petra tou Romiou (Aphrodite's birthplace). There are plenty of places to park at the picnic site.

This short nature trail takes you to the mythological birthplace of Aphrodite. The goddess of love rose from the sea near Paphos after Cronos cut off Uranus' genitals and threw them into the water.

The pebble beach with the famous sea stack is therefore a popular destination, but most people arrive by car or bus and miss the trail on the coast. As you follow the coastline you will be treated with fine coastal views.

From the map board, take the track that skirts around the picnic site. Shortly after the start you can enjoy some fine views towards the sea. The trail runs fairly close to the B6 road and there are some tracks/paths joining from the left, but stay on the well-trodden track. You will occasionally see some walker signs as well. At around 1km you have the first glimpse of the famous sea stack in the distance.

Ignore the other tracks and keep closer to the sea, which is on your right.

The track comes close to the road and then descends slightly towards the beach. At 2km the path splits; keep left (you will return to this junction from the beach from the path on the right).

Get close to the road again and head to the nearby viewpoint. From there you can enjoy some fine views towards the beach and sea stack.

From this viewpoint cross the road, and the nature trail continues on its other side, and shortly after veers away from the road. When the track splits go right for better views (the paths will rejoin). Enjoy some further views to the coast and a few minutes later at the junction, keep right downhill. And then take the first path

WALK 5 – PETRA TOU ROMIOU NATURE TRAIL

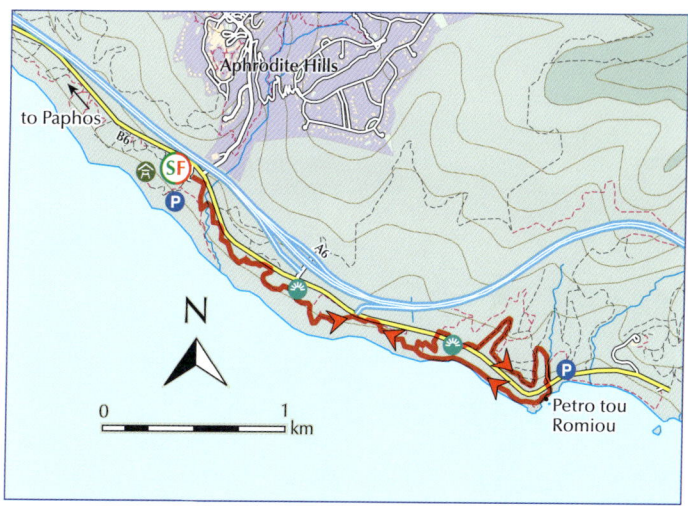

The scenic coastline leads the eye to Aphrodite's birthplace

Signs with names identify certain plants along the route

on the right that leads down to a parking area. (The nature trail continues to the next hill to another lookout point and then reaches the car park from there). Walk across the parking area and go through the underpass to the beach.

Keep right and walk along the pebble beach. Walk below the viewpoint and at the end of the beach join the track and this time with the sea on your left retrace your steps to the **picnic site**.

> Petra tou Romiou, also known as Aphrodite's Rock, is a sea stack near the shore, where according to the legend, Aphrodite, as an adult, rose from foaming waters.

WALK 6
Horteri Nature Trail

Start/finish	Locality Platanouthkia, east of Stavros tis Psokas (N35.02503, E32.63483)
Distance	5km
Total ascent/descent	460m/460m
Grade	1
Time	1hr 30min–2hr
Refreshments	The nearest is in Stavros tis Psokas
Access	Locality Platanouthkia is about 2km east from Stavros tis Psokas on the F723 road. The drive to the start of the trail involves countless hairpin bends on a quiet and dramatic road. Parking available on roadside.

A short, peaceful and spectacular nature trail in the shade of trees with impressive views of endless forest-covered hills. The first half of the trail – on part of the E4 – climbs steadily uphill, and then the route descends on a narrow footpath.

Paphos Forest is home to over 600 different plant species. The Cyprus cedar can only be found here, and it is especially typical around Tripylos Mountain. There is a mouflon enclosure at Stavros tis Psokas, located only 2km from the beginning of the trail, providing an opportunity to see these endemic animals.

Walk up the stone steps behind the roadside fountain. The path runs uphill for a few minutes and then splits; go sharply left, uphill as the E4 sign indicates. You will arrive back at this junction at end of the walk.

Climb steeply uphill on the narrow, stony path beneath trees and then zig-zag on the hillside with views to the forest-covered mountains. As you ascend between golden oaks and moss-covered rocks, it is possible to spot the roofs of the houses of the forest station and a helipad in the distance. About 15min after turning left at the intersection you arrive at the first of several benches designated as special viewpoints, from where the Stavros river valley near the forest station and the Zacharou fire lookout station on a distant hilltop can be seen on a clear day. Soon the path takes a sharp U-turn to the right and continues uphill with mountain views now on the right. About 1hr into the walk you reach the **Locality Horteri** sign at 1215m.

WALKING IN CYPRUS

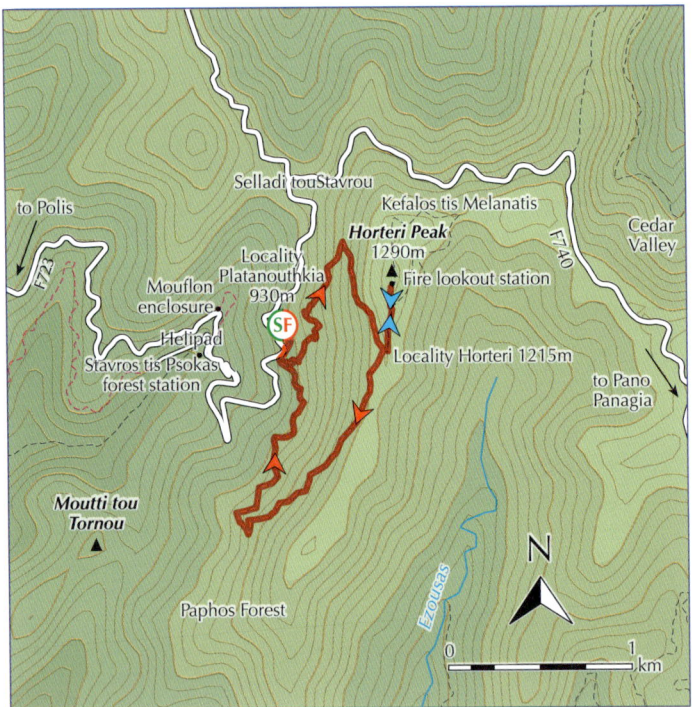

The main trail continues downhill beneath trees, slightly to the right, but first there is an option to climb to the top of Horteri. The ascent path is not clearly marked and the summit, with a huge antenna, fire lookout platform and the ruins of a building, might be a bit disappointing – but the views are great. Allow 25min return.

Optional ascent of Horteri
From Locality Horteri, take the wider path marked 'E4', slightly uphill on the left. Follow the wide path for 5–7min and as the track bends to the right the antenna on top of Horteri comes into sight. It is a long way on the forest track to get to the top, so you might consider a short-cut here: just when the forest track bends right, slightly downhill, there is a clearing on the left-hand side, and if you carefully observe the bushes you will see a stone cairn. An overgrown but distinguishable

path leads straight to the top. From here it takes 5–6min to get to the summit between shrubs.

From the **summit** there are scenic views towards the Cedar Valley, Troodos mountains and Chrysochou Bay; admire the panorama and then retrace your steps back to the Locality Horteri sign and the junction with the bench.

Main trail

To continue on the main trail, go slightly downhill: coming from Horteri's summit it is the path on the left; if you didn't go to the top it is the path on the right. The very narrow path runs along the hillside with views now on the right. Moss-covered trees often obstruct the views but there are plenty of viewpoints along the descent. About 40min into the descent, the path makes a sudden U-turn to the right and soon the road comes into view. Reach the junction with the E4 sign where you took the other branch earlier. Go downhill and a few minutes later arrive back at **Locality Platanouthkia**.

Descend on a narrow path through dense pine forest

WALK 7
Vouni path

Start/finish	Pano Panagia (N34.91832, E32.63142)
Distance	8.5km; via the monastery: 10.5km
Total ascent/descent	290m; via the monastery: 335m
Grade	2
Time	2hr 30min–3hr; via the monastery: 3hr 40min (+ allow extra time to visit the monastery)
Refreshments	Pano Panagia
Access	Pano Panagia is located on the E606 road, which can be accessed from the B6. There are daily buses from Paphos.

This route follows meandering, occasionally steep dirt roads through well-maintained old vineyards. The track meets several other tracks wriggling between the cultivated land, but the Vouni path is easy to follow and there are signs at every junction. Excellent panoramas can be enjoyed throughout this trail and visiting the Chrysorrogiatissa Monastery with its relaxing atmosphere can complete the day perfectly. The monks make their own wine; don't miss the opportunity to buy a bottle.

The trail starts by the information board in Pano Panagia.

Pano Panagia is the birthplace of Archbishop Makarios III (1913–1977), the first president of the Republic of Cyprus from 1960 until his death in 1977.

Start on the tarmac road (Agiou Georgiou) that runs steeply uphill by a vineyard. The Vouni path is clearly signposted and, as with most nature trails, many plants are labelled along the way. After ascending for about 10min, at an intersection take the wide, stony track on the right. Soon there are views to Pano Panagia village and a few minutes later there is an opportunity to admire the panorama from a **viewpoint** located on the right, clearly visible from the road bend.

From the roofed **viewing platform** you can spot the Triplos and Moutti tous Anemous mountain peaks, among many others, as well as Kannaviou Dam in the distance, while listening to the echoes from Panagia.

WALK 7 – VOUNI PATH

Chrysorrogiatissa Monastery

From the viewpoint retrace your steps to the road bend and continue uphill between terraced vineyards. Tracks adjoin the stony trail but there are signs indicating the right direction. Reach an information board about the unique Cyprus vegetation about 20min after the viewpoint; from here the track climbs vigorously uphill and then runs between vineyards again. There are fine views to the mountains of Troodos before you pass a **fire lookout station** at 1135m, about 20min after the information board.

Just after the fire lookout building the track levels out a bit. Continue between vineyards and then shortly reach the second viewpoint, from where you can spot Chrysorrogiatissa Monastery. Continue on the track and soon arrive at **Profitis Elias Chapel**, from where you start to descend.

At the first junction after the church go right, and at the next intersection bear left. There are some rocks and bushes around the dirt track but soon – once again – the scenery is dominated by vineyards.

Keep right at the next two junctions. The track swings steadily downhill with views to cultivated slopes with mountains in the background and you can even spot Agios Moni down

57

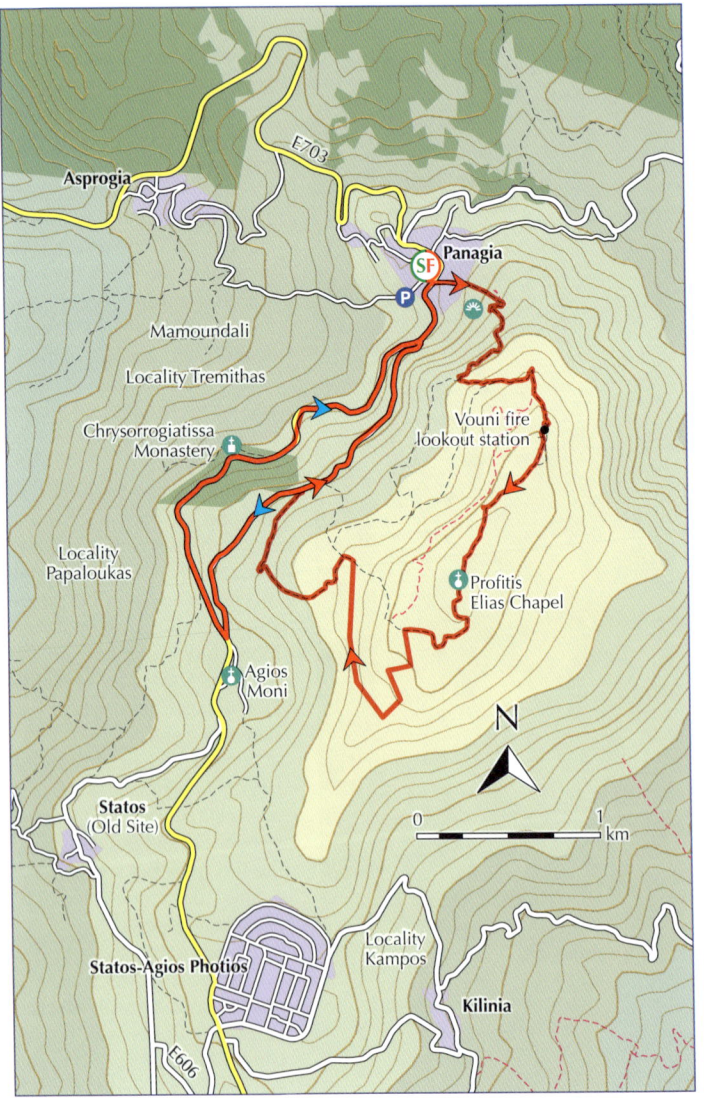

WALK 7 – VOUNI PATH

Wonderful views can be enjoyed towards the surrounding mountains

on the left. At the intersection before a water tank, go right as an arrow indicates. Soon, as you descend steeply, the houses of Pano Panagia come into view.

To visit Chrysorrogiatissa Monastery

To visit the monastery, turn left at the junction with a sign to Panagia and Chrysorrogiatissa Monastery. It is 1km on a tarmac road to reach the main road, where you turn right and walk a further 1km to reach the **monastery**. From there it is another 1.5km on the tarmac road back to **Panagia** village.

> The **Chrysorrogiatissa Monastery** was founded in 1152. Monk Ignatios found an icon of the Virgin Mary near Paphos, and built a monastery in the mountains, dedicated to 'Our Lady of the Golden Pomegranate'. The present building – home to a collection of icons – dates back to 1770. The monastery's old winery makes some fine wines from grapes grown in its vineyards.

Alternatively, rather than following the sign to Chrysorrogiatissa Monastery, you can walk straight back to **Panagia** (1.5km) on the tarmac road on the right.

WALK 8
Zalakas Trail

Start/finish	Trimiklini, Panagia Eleousa old and Panagia Eleousa new churches (N34.846060, E32.910598)
Distance	8.5km
Total ascent/descent	260m
Grad	1
Time	2hr 30min
Refreshments	None along the trail. Restaurant, shop and café/bar in Trimiklini.
Access	Trimiklini is located along the B8 road between Limassol and Pano Platres. There is a car park near the churches.

The first section of the nature trail runs through an area that was devastated by fire that affected 1.5 square kilometres near the village. But as you climb away from the village you can enjoy some great views towards the Troodos mountains. North of Trimiklini you will find the double bridge that was constructed at the beginning of the 20th century to provide better transport connection between Trimiklini and Pera Pedi villages.

The track leading out of the village

WALK 8 – ZALAKAS TRAIL

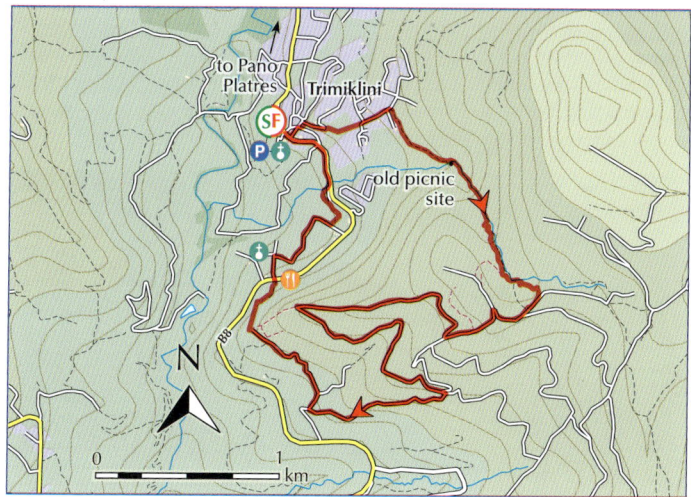

From the B8 road take the street (opposite the church) up between the Cultural centre and a small supermarket. Follow this road, then turn left and then the road bends right among houses. Leaving the tarmac lane in a bend of a road, continue on a track straight on. A walker sign marks this. A few minutes later reach a tarmac lane and follow the track straight on by a house. The landscape wears a burnt scar, but there are great views of the Troodos mountains. At around 1km arrive at a **picnic area** (at the time of writing it is destroyed by fire).

Continue on the wide path that runs on the terraced hillside and before long walk alongside the streambed. As you ascend occasionally there is a handrail by the path. When the path splits you can take either branch as soon they will rejoin. One runs on a lower level closer to the streambed and the other one higher up but they will rejoin near a bench.

At 2km, reach a dirt track and go right. For the next couple of kilometres you will follow this track steadily downhill with views of the mountains of Troodos. Another track joins from the left and then at the track junction keep right. On the left you can see the houses of Laneia. At the next junction go right. You bear right again at the next junction and then shortly after keep left as the walker sign indicates the route. About an hour after you joined the track it comes to an end and you continue downhill on a path. As you descend you can spot a reservoir on the left. The path runs above the road parallel to it. Reach the B8 road, opposite a restaurant.

Cross over and continue downhill among cultivated lands. There is a small **church** on the left but the trail continues to the right. Pass a house and shortly after - just before you would reach the road - go left on a narrow path, which has cultivated land nearby. The path becomes surfaced and leads back to the B8 road. Go left and walk back to the **church**, which is only a few minutes away.

The old Panagia Eleousa church in Trimiklini Village

THE TROODOS AND CENTRAL CYPRUS

Narrow street in Kakopetria

Views towards the second highest peak, Madari in the distance (Walk 13)

Troodos is cooler than the coast and many of its trails can be enjoyed at most times of the year. In the winter, snow can cover the highest parts of the Troodos and its ski slopes are visited by winter sports enthusiasts.

Troodos Square is usually bustling with tourists but you can start some spectacular trails from there – and after your walk you can buy local products in the souvenir shops and have a meal in one of the restaurants. For those who want to learn more about Troodos, the Troodos Visitor Centre, located just outside of Troodos Square, is worth a visit. The village of Pano Platres – about 8km from Troodos Square – has some hotels and restaurants, and can be a great base for people who want to explore the trails in the area.

Winding roads connect the quiet villages where Byzantine monasteries and small churches are hidden on the pine-covered slopes. A section of the long-distance E4 trail connects two UNESCO-listed churches, and you can find some charming trails near the grand Machairas Monastery. Many of the region's trails give an opportunity to visit a church or monastery or a charismatic village.

Kakopetria on the banks of the Karkotis river – where Cypriots from Nicosia own holiday homes to escape the summer heat – is another peaceful base for walkers.

WALK 9
Marathasa Trail

Start/finish	E912 road junction 3km west of Pedoulas (N 34.975501 E 32.809316)
Distance	12.5km
Total ascent/descent	700m
Grade	3
Time	4hr 30min
Refreshments	Water tap with non-potable water at Xystarouda picnic site
Access	The start/finish point is located at a road junction along the E912, about 3km west of Pedoulas. You will need your own transport or arrange a taxi.

The trail described follows one of the five numbered trails in the Marathasa Valley area. This trail follows Route 5, also known as the Discovery Trail. It starts with a descent to a valley where you follow a stream (or stream bed) through forest. After the climb to Xystarouda picnic site, the second part of the route follows scenic ridges with some excellent views of the forest-covered mountains.

At the road junction a map board and signpost marks the start of Route 5. Go downhill on the narrow path, with views of forested mountains; you might be able to make out Kykkos Monastery in the distance. Soon descend through forest and just after 1km into the walk (15min from start) pass a small **stone building/shelter**. The path continues downhill and widens as you reach the bottom of the valley and it then runs alongside a (dry) streambed. During the next 20min you cross the streambed myriad times.

You might notice when the forest floor becomes more lush and there is a small stream with trickling water by the path. Cross the stream on rocks twice and then continue alongside it, reaching a junction with a signpost. Go right uphill on the path towards Xystarouda picnic site. As you ascend pass the site of the **settlement** of Ano Platys on the hill. It is nothing more than some rocks scattered around the hill. The path descends slightly and then runs on the mountainside.

Great views over the Marathasa valley on the final section of the trail

After a climb reach the **Xystarouda picnic site**, which is located next to the E912 road.

This could be an alternative starting point, as there are places to park. It is about halfway on the route and perhaps a great stop for a picnic. (There are plenty of picnic tables, toilets and also a tap but the water is non-potable.)

Cross the road and then the route continues by the information/map board (this is also the start of Walk 10). Go down on steps and then descend for about 20min to reach a **path junction** with a signpost and benches. (From this junction Walk 10 goes left and you can make a short detour to the fountain.) Go right uphill between two benches, and as you follow the narrow ridge, mountains fill the horizon in both directions. Now you can see Kykkos Monastery and you might also spot the picnic site by the road as you follow the contour of the mountainside for about 30min.

Dense forest in the bottom of the valley

WALK 9 – MARATHASA TRAIL

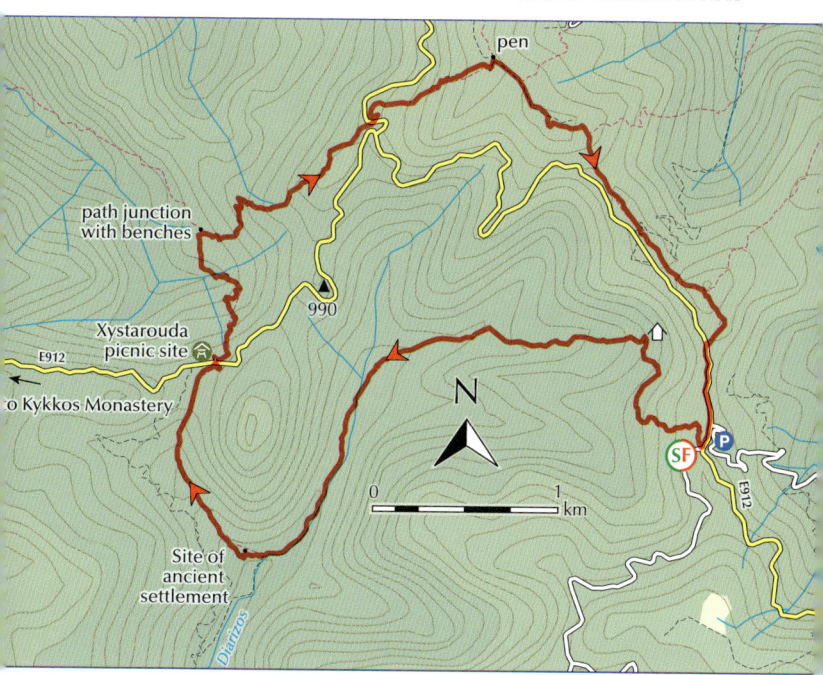

Notice the snaking tarmac lane and shortly after reach the road by the trail map, cross over and continue on the path on its other side uphill. Initially it runs parallel to the road but then it veers away and you walk with a valley and mountain on your right. Ascend through forest and reach a track, go left and almost immediately at the track junction keep right (towards Xylogefyro). Shortly after at the path junction near a **pen** continue straight on with some views towards Gerakies on the left. Leave this track to the right on a path marked with a trail sign, and climb up to another ridge. There are trigpoints located along this ridge, many with trail signs on them. Descend to a path junction with a signpost and carry straight on downhill towards Xylogefyro. Route 4 and Route 5 run together on this section so you might see both signs. Cross a track and continue on its other side. You can enjoy some excellent views from this rocky ridge and then zigzag up to another trigpoint. At the path junction with signs, keep right and descend on a narrow path – often on a loose surface – to the road. Go left and follow the road back to the junction/starting point, only a few minutes away.

WALK 10
Xystarouda – Agiasma – Vasiliki Nature Trail

Start/finish	Xystarouda picnic site (N34.97940, E32.77986)
Distance	12km
Total ascent/descent	660m
Grade	2
Time	5hr
Refreshments	Tap (non-potable water) at Xystarouda picnic site
Access	Xystarouda picnic site is on the E912 road approximately halfway between Gerakies village and Kykkos Monastery. There are places to park at the picnic site.

This there-and-back route follows an undulating path in a peaceful forest where you may spot mouflon hopping nimbly on rocks. After descending to a valley where a small stream is hidden by trees, it climbs steeply uphill with splendid views to the mountains. At the end of the trail you arrive at the small St Vasilios church encircled by mountains. As on many nature trails, you will most probably have to retrace your steps back to the picnic site.

MOUFLON

The Cyprus mouflon – a shy, light brown wild sheep – is the largest mammal in Cyprus. The male is slightly bigger than the female and can be recognised by its heavy, sickle-shaped horns. During the summer months the mouflon skilfully hop on the steep slopes of Paphos Forest in search of food. However, in the winter when the mountains might be covered with snow they live at a lower altitude.

Roman mosaics provide evidence that mouflon were around in Roman times. Aristocrats hunted them during the Middle Ages, and when the use of guns for hunting became widespread, their numbers decreased significantly.

Today, Paphos Forest is a Special Protected Area and thanks to the great effort to protect the mouflon and their habitat, their numbers have returned to a satisfactory level.

WALK 10 – XYSTAROUDA – AGIASMA – VASILIKI NATURE TRAIL

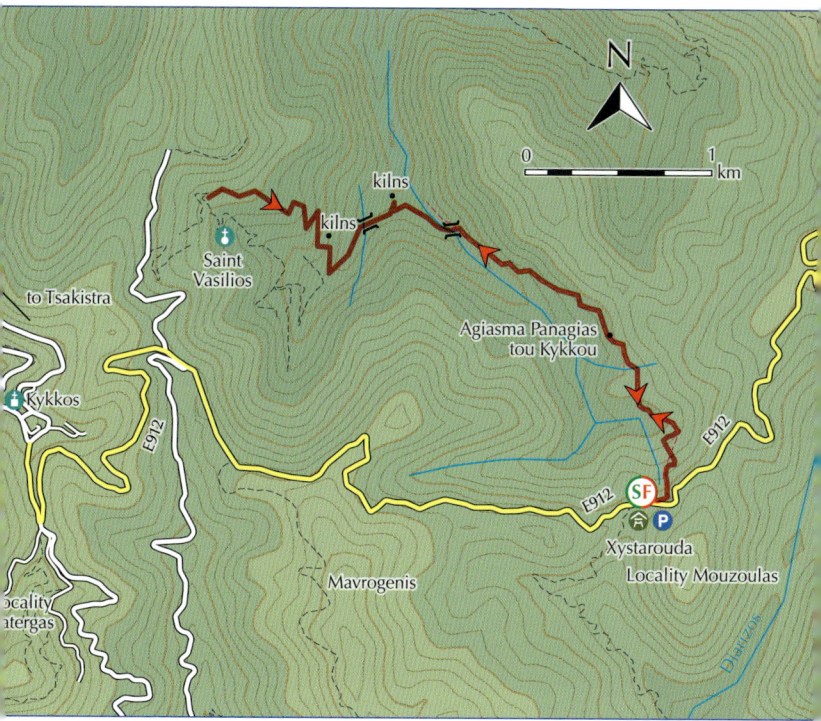

The path starts opposite the picnic site, by the map board. There are steps leading steeply downhill between golden oaks, and soon some views to the mountains on the left. The well-trodden nature trail is clear and easy to follow. Pine trees and golden oaks are the main vegetation as the path swings around the mountainside, heading constantly downhill for 20min to a path junction with a signpost and benches. Go left and descend for another 15min to arrive at **Agiasma Panagias tou Kykkou** (spring). The spring is a small pool in the rock at the foot of the rock wall.

Agiasma means 'holy water'. The **spring** is believed to have appeared miraculously from the rocks and many people visit the site. Small pieces of cloth hang from a nearby tree and there are images on the wall indicating that for many this is a special place.

A small wooden bridge connects the banks of the rushing stream

Continue downhill on intermittent steps with great views to the mountains, and about 10min after the spring, note an ancient olive tree on your left-hand side. As you descend, you'll soon hear the gurgling water from the valley on your left. Lush vegetation indicates the presence of the water and about 20-25min after the spring you arrive at a small rushing stream.

Cross the wooden **bridge** and the fern-enveloped path continues by the waterway. Soon start ascending, with views to the gorge and the rocky mountain slope on its opposite side. As the path bends away from the valley through which the stream flows, it runs beneath very tall pine trees. About 15min after the bridge, the path splits; the right branch takes you to a **kiln** approximately 60m away and the other branch is the main trail.

Continue along the mountainside and shortly you will hear the sound of gurgling water again. After a short descent, arrive at a second **bridge**. The path is only close to the stream for a few metres before it crawls steeply uphill. Walk along the hillside with the gorge on the left and soon climb steeply uphill again.

About 20min after the second bridge, pass some old **kilns** and then continue uphill. Soon, as you're ascending, you will spot Mt Olympus in the Troodos in the distance on your left and some olive plantations down in the valley. When the path starts to descend, note some houses and the old Saint Vasilios church in the valley. Continue downhill and arrive at an information board at a road. To visit the **church** (open 8am–12midday and 3.30pm–5pm), turn left and walk about 300m along the road.

After visiting the church, retrace your steps back to **Xystarouda picnic site**.

WALK 11
Prodromos Dam – Stavroulia Trail

Start/finish	Prodromos Dam picnic site (N34.94755, E32.84712)
Distance	9.5km
Total ascent/descent	275m
Grade	1
Time	3hr
Refreshments	None on route; restaurant in Prodromos
Access	Prodromos Dam picnic site is located on the Troodos–Prodromos (F952) road, 2.5km from Prodromos village. Parking space available.

This walk combines the best of the Prodromos – Zoumi and Prodromos – Stavroulia nature trails. It is made circular by walking on the asphalt road for about 3.5km at the end of the walk. There are viewpoints along the way where you can take time to enjoy the stunning views towards Morfou Bay, the mountains and Kykkos Monastery. Detailed nature trail labels help to identify many of the plants on this trail.

Prodromos' (1380m) cooler climate in the summer and the closeness of the ski resorts on Mt Olympus have been attracting visitors for many years. The once-luxurious Berengaria Hotel, formerly frequented by royalty, lies near the village. It opened in 1931 but was abandoned in 1984. According to local legend it is haunted by ghosts. Plans were made for restoration, however the grand building is still slowly decaying.

From the picnic site, the trail starts beneath black pine trees by the information board on the right-hand side of the road from the direction of Troodos. Walk downhill on the stony path, which soon levels out and runs on the hillside between prickly junipers and Cyprus cedars. The path soon heads along a railing with views towards Pedoulas village with a Balkan war memorial on the slope encircled by mountains. Trees are sparse on the stony mountainside, giving plenty of opportunity to marvel at the panorama.

Start to descend with excellent views towards Morfou Bay about 40–45min from the start of the walk. Soon spot a path to the right going to a viewpoint which is only a few metres away. Continue descending on the loose, stony ground with

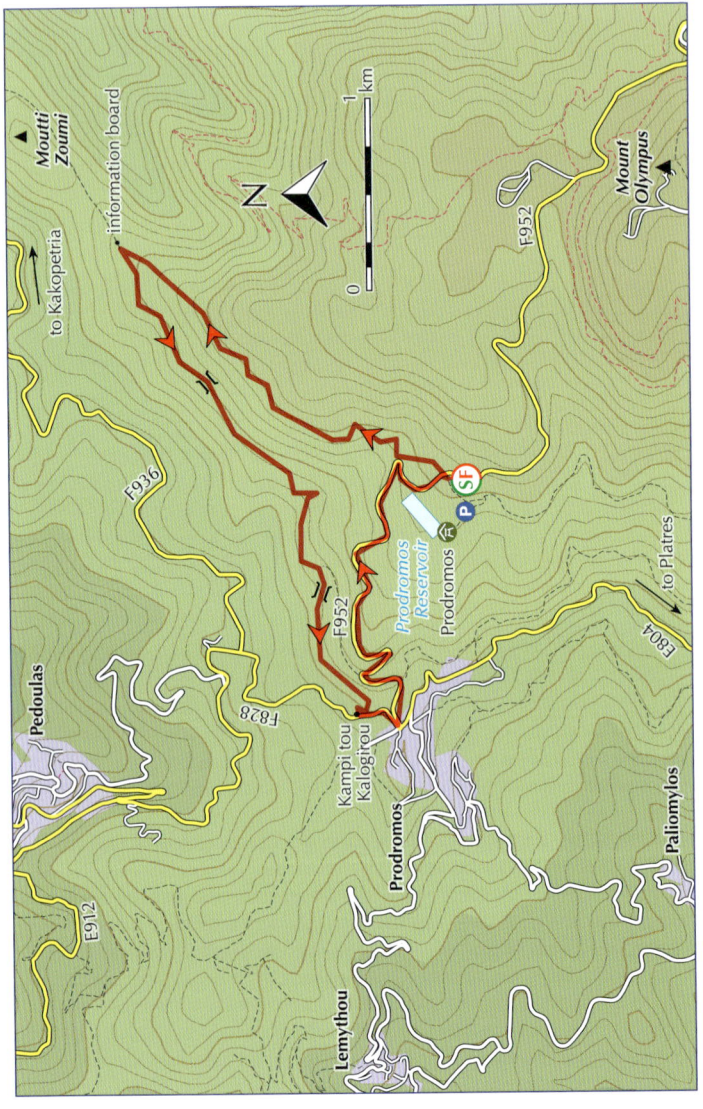

Dried-out tree: one of many natural 'statues' scattered on the mountainside

views towards the Kyrenia range, and after a very steep downhill section arrive at a junction with an **information board**.

Continue left, uphill beneath pine trees. At first the views are obstructed by the trees and bushes but soon Pedoulas village and the surrounding mountains appear on your right.

Follow the path with enchanting views for about 20min and arrive at a small wooden **bridge**. Continue on the undulating path for another 20min or so. When the path splits, keep right and a few minutes later arrive at a dirt track with a blank information board. Go left on the dirt track and about 10min later leave it to the right on a path downhill.

Soon cross another wooden **bridge**. You might notice a faint path on the right, but keep straight on the well-trodden path and then some buildings (**Kampi tou Kalogirou**) appear on the right. Soon pass by a playground; there is a restaurant to the left on the other side of the road. Arrive at an information board and go left on the asphalt road (F828). Walk past the restaurant and at the roundabout go towards Troodos (F952 road). Follow the winding asphalt road for 3.5km to arrive back at **Prodromos Dam picnic site**.

WALK 12
Kannoures Trail

Start	800m from Agios Nikolaos tis Stegis church on the F936 road (N34.97791, E32.88517)
Finish	Troodos Square
Distance	10km
Total ascent/descent	960m/115m
Grade	3
Time	3hr–3hr 30min
Refreshments	Restaurants and shops in Troodos Square
Access	From the direction of Troodos village on the B9 road, before reaching Kakopetria, turn left onto F936. Follow this winding road to Agios Nikolaos tis Stegis church. (It is possible to park in the church car park but check the opening hours (see below), as the gate is shut outside of visiting times.) From the church, follow the tarmac (F936) road for about 800m. There is space for parking by the nature trail sign at the beginning of the walk.
Note	The walk is intended as a one-way route; it is best to arrange a taxi from Troodos Square back to the start point before setting out.

Like a secret gem, the gorge that holds the Karkotis river is hidden by the mountains of Troodos. For a number of kilometres the scenery on this walk is dominated by rocks, pine trees, boulders and the river. The path crosses the rushing stream countless times, often on slippery rocks, in the picturesque gorge. There is the possibility of seeing the endemic mouflon hopping on rocks, and birds swooping between pine trees, as you make your way through this magical ravine.

AGIOS NIKOLAOS TIS STEGIS

Also known as 'St Nicholas of the Roof', its name refers to the second timber roof which was added to protect the building from snow. The Byzantine church was part of a monastery built in the 11th century; the narthex, dome

and second roof were added a few hundred years later. Apart from the church, no other buildings of the monastery survived.

Wall paintings – dating from at least five different centuries – cover the entire interior and the church is listed as a UNESCO World Heritage Site.

Visiting hours: Tuesday–Saturday, 9am–4pm; Sunday, 11am–4pm; closed on Mondays and public holidays.

The trail starts as a wide forest track on the left side of the F936 road about 800m from Agios Nikolaos tis Stegis church. The start is marked with a 'Nature Trail Agios Nikolaos – Kannoures 9km' sign.

The wide forest track winds uphill on the mountainside with views to Kakopetria on the left. Pass by a fenced area where you can see some of the old buildings of a former mine in the valley. Ascend on the track with some views and

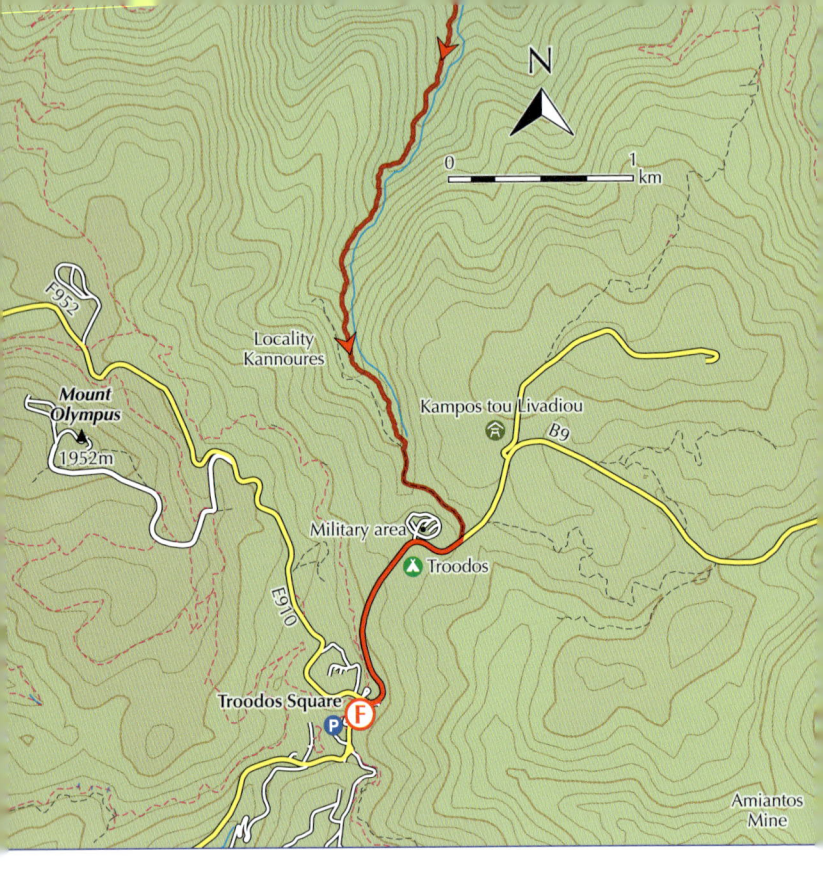

about 40min after leaving the tarmac road go left on the narrow path by a bench. A sign marks the path.

Follow this footpath on the mountainside with occasional views to the surrounding rocky mountains. Curve around rocks with views to a captivating ravine on the left and soon walk between boulders closer to the rushing stream. About half an hour after leaving the wide dirt track, cross the stream for the first time and then climb steadily uphill by the river. A giant rock towers on the right as the rocky path makes its way deeper into the gorge.

Less than 10min after the first crossing, cross the stream again. For nearly two hours you will follow the stream on the rough footpath and cross the water myriad times. The crossings are often on slippery rocks; select your crossing points carefully because the water is deep and the flow can be rapid in places.

The rugged path runs steadily uphill. Pine trees are the main vegetation in the gorge, but sometimes they are completely absent, leaving only the barren mountainside and the sound of rushing water. The narrow path is easy to follow but occasionally you may have to alter your way and walk upstream a bit to find a better crossing place.

As you zigzag uphill around the 5km mark, stop and look back to admire a scenic panorama of the plains and the beginning of the Kyrenia range. From around the 6km mark there are more pine trees clinging onto the rocky mountainside.

A small rushing waterfall in the picturesque gorge

The Karkotis river is crossed several times

The path winds relentlessly uphill with huge rocks on the left. Continue climbing and cross the stream a few more times before a wide forest track becomes visible on the other side of the streambed. Soon the path bends right, crosses the river and joins a forest track. Turn left and follow the rugged forest track. Pass by some young pine trees and reach the tarmac road (B9). Turn right and follow this road for 1.2km to arrive at **Troodos Square**, from where you can either retrace your steps (although this would make a very long outing) or take a taxi back to the start.

WALK 13
Mnimata Piskopon Trail

Start	Kampos tou Livadiou picnic site (N34.93607, E32.88959)
Finish	Agios Nikolaos tis Stegis church
Distance	10km
Total ascent/descent	130m/960m
Grade	2
Time	3hr–3hr 30min
Refreshments	None along the way. Cafés and restaurants in Troodos Square.
Access	The nature trail starts on the left side of the B9 road about 1.5km from Troodos Square towards Karvounas. Parking available nearby.
Note	This is intended as a one-way route; while retracing your steps from Agios Nikolaos tis Stegis is possible, it would make a long day with a steep climb on the return. It is best to arrange a taxi before setting out.

The first section of this walk follows a very well-maintained nature trail offering excellent views to Mt Olympus – Cyprus' highest peak. The narrow path beneath pine trees occasionally joins forest tracks, and after a leisurely start it goes steeply downhill on loose ground. As you descend you will have breathtaking views towards Kakopetria village, the Madari ridge and Morphou Bay.

The trail starts just off the B9 road, where there is space to park. The Mnimata Piskopon Trail and the E4 trail follow the tarmac lane towards Platania for about 500m passing the trailhead of the Livadi Trail. Go left on the track. Follow the E4 trail through forest downhill. Ignore a track on the right and follow the E4 trail straight on. At around 1km ignore a path on the left and continue on the forest track downhill with views to pine-dotted rocky mountainsides and the first glimpse of the distant Adelfoi (Madari) peak. There are occasional E4 marks on some trees, and about 40-45min from the start the E4 leaves the track to the right. This is a short-cut as a few minutes later it rejoins the track, where you keep

WALK 13 – MNIMATA PISKOPON TRAIL

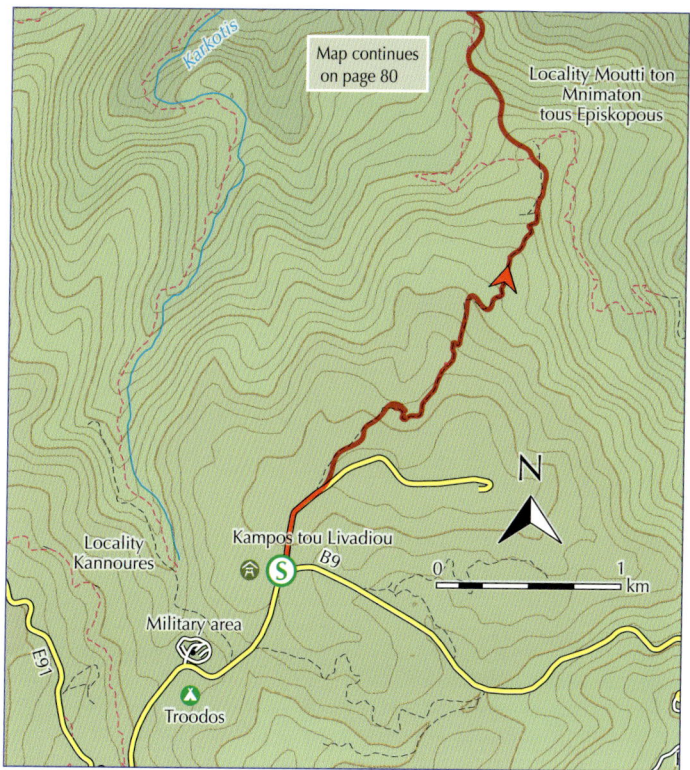

right. At a junction where the E4 heads to Platania, fork left towards Kakopetria. From here the path runs steeply downhill. You will see the remains of some steps, and the ground is very loose and slippery as you descend. There are views to Mt Olympus on the left and soon you have a direct view to Kakopetria, a football pitch, Cape Kormakitis and Morphou Bay.

About 20min after leaving the E4 trail, arrive at a dirt track. Keep right downhill and about 70m later the path leaves the forest road to the right by a bench. Continue downhill on a very steep, rough and loose path with some deteriorated steps and then walk in the shade of trees for a while. Descend steeply for about 45min, mainly on stony, crumbly ground with excellent views to the mountains and Kakopetria.

Not long before reaching a dirt road the path becomes sandy with scattered stones. Arrive at the dirt road with 'Agios Nikolaos 3km' and 'Platania 5km' signs. Go left towards Agios Nikolaos and at the next junction keep straight on. Follow the 'number 1' cycle route, which goes in the same direction for about 1.8km.

Ignore the track on the right as you arrive at a bench and a **cycle route map**. About 250m later, when the track turns right, spot 'hideout 1&2' signs on the left. You can make a detour to visit one of them via a small path on a bend. Soon after a bend the cycle route leaves the track to the right; continue straight on and 500m later arrive at a **trout farm building** where you cross the rushing Karkotis river. About 700m later you reach the end of the dirt track; go right on the concrete road and follow it to the Agios Nikolaos tis Stegis church.

The Byzantine **Agios Nikolaos tis Stegis church** was part of a monastery built in the 11th century; its narthex, dome and second roof were added a few hundred years later. The church is the only surviving building of the monastery complex, and its interior wall paintings have won it a place on the UNESCO World Heritage List.

Walk 13 – Mnimata Piskopon Trail

Descend on a narrow rocky path with great views on the surrounding landscape

Visiting hours: Tuesday–Saturday, 9am–4pm; Sunday, 11am–4pm; closed on Mondays and public holidays.

Having visited the church you can either retrace your steps (bearing in mind that this would involve a steep climb) or follow Walk 12 (Kannoures Trail) or take a taxi back to the **picnic site** at the start.

WALK 14
Atalante Trail

Start/finish	Troodos Square (N34.92424, E32.88082)
Distance	14km
Total ascent/descent	325m
Grade	2
Time	4hr–4hr 30min
Refreshments	Restaurants and souvenir shops on Troodos Square
Access	Troodos Square can be accessed from the B8 and B9 roads. There is a large car park at the start point.

A well-signposted, narrow, stony path cut into a mountainside runs around Mt Olympus, with impressive views along the way. It is a comfortable walk beneath pines and without strenuous ascent. Despite the length of the trail, many people take it to admire the panorama. Yet there are sections where you find yourself alone and can enjoy the rustling trees and birdsong. This walk is most enjoyable on a clear day.

> **Atalante** is a renowned and swift-footed huntress in Greek mythology. Her father wanted a son, and when she was born she was left in the woods to die. However, Atalante was found and looked after by a bear. Growing up, she spent lot of time with hunters and became the best of them.

The signposted trail starts at the end of the boardwalk by the playground next to the main road. The well-trodden path runs beneath pine trees on the hillside and soon past the **Jubilee Hotel** on the right. Cross a dry streambed and continue to the left, passing the **Troodos Visitor Centre** from above.

The well-used, narrow – sometimes exposed – path continues on the side of Mt Olympus with a rock wall towering on the right. The snaking road between Platres and Troodos is on the left down below and there are stunning views towards the south coast.

After the 2km mark the vegetation becomes denser and you walk between bushes and pine trees for a while. About 30–40min after leaving Troodos Square, the narrow footpath meets another path; continue straight on by a bench with an iron arrow indicating the direction.

WALK 14 – ATALANTE TRAIL

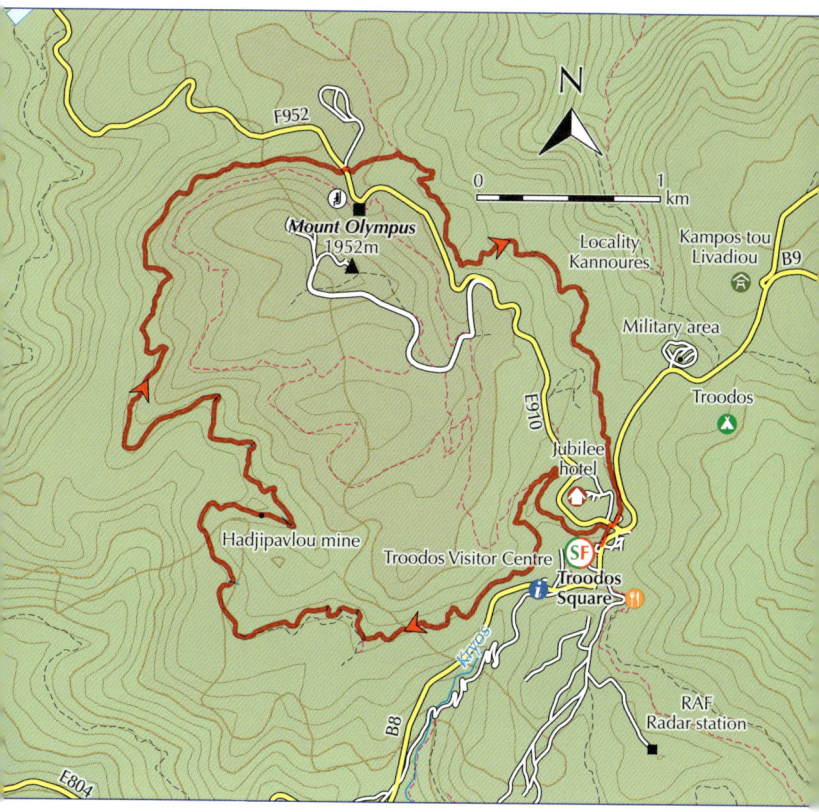

Pine trees obstruct the view for a while. Cross a little stream and then arrive at a fountain with running water at the 3km mark. After the fountain there is a clear view again on the left and a sheer rocky mountainside scattered with pine trees towering on the right. Soon spot a terraced reforestation area on the far left, as well as the tops of the two radar domes on a nearby mountain. About 20min after the fountain the path joins into a wider track; keep right and soon the track narrows back into a path.

Follow the contour of the mountainside with fantastic views on the left and a rocky slope soaring on the right, and then at around the 5km mark the path arrives at the disused **Hadjipavlou chromium mine**.

Entrance of the closed Hadjipavlou mine

The **mine** has been closed since 1982 and there is a fence in front of the entrance. The roof of the tunnel has collapsed in places, but standing at the entrance you can feel the cold, damp air drifting out.

After the mine as you continue by a rock face you might hear a thin gurgling stream on your left down below. Soon another path joins in; keep left, cross a stream and then walk by pines and cypress trees. As the path sharply doubles back on itself, look back to see the entrance of the mine. The trail is exposed in places as it swings around rocks.

Soon the view slightly changes, and on the left the distant houses of Prodromos dominate the panorama as you walk through pine forest. At around the 8km mark you'll see the top of Mt Olympus on the right, and 1km later as you walk by juniper trees the road is clearly visible.

The path widens and soon arrives at a noticeboard and a stone building by a tarmac road. Cross the road by the information board. There is a parking area slightly to your right; head towards the electricity pole and the trail continues on a dirt track to the left.

MT OLYMPUS

Rocky path on the southern side of Mount Olympus

Mt Olympus (known locally as Chionistra – 'the snowy one') at 1952m is the highest mountain in Cyprus. Its highest point can't be accessed as a British long-range radar operates from its peak. However, some of the most popular and enjoyable trails with magnificent views are on its pine-covered mountainside. Europe's most southerly ski resorts are on Mt Olympus' slopes. People started skiing in Cyprus in 1934, and in 1947 the Cyprus Ski Club was established. After a first ski lift on the eastern side of the mountain, the second ski lift started operating west of Troodos in 1951.

Walk with a drop on your right, noting a building on the hill on the left. A few minutes later leave the track on a narrow path to the right and descend into a ravine, and then ascend on occasional stone steps. At the 12km mark the path joins a dirt track; continue downhill to the left as an iron arrow indicates.

Walk on the mountainside with the ravine on your left and about 600m later another forest track joins in. Keep right as an arrow indicates. Down below on the left an impressive gorge can be seen with the hidden Kannoures trail, and in the distance Kakopetria village. Leave the dirt track to the right as an arrow indicates and about 15min later arrive back at **Troodos Square**.

WALK 15
Artemis Trail

Start/finish	Troodos Square (N34.92424, E32.88082)
Alternative start/finish	Car park on the F953 road (N34.93304, E32.87216)
Distance	12km; from alternative start (official Artemis Trail): 7km
Total ascent/descent	215m; from alternative start: 170m
Grade	2; from alternative start: 1
Time	3hr 40min; from alternative start: 2hr 30min
Refreshments	Cafés and restaurants at Troodos Square
Access	Troodos Square can be accessed from the B8 and B9 roads. Alternative start is on the F953 road about 300m from the Troodos–Prodromos road (E910). There is a large car park at the start point.

Like an older sister, the Artemis Trail looks over to the Atalante Trail from a higher altitude. The trail is considerably shorter than the Atalante Trail; however, by starting from Troodos Square, first briefly following the Atalante Trail and then joining the Artemis Trail after about 2km, the distance is lengthened to 12km. The signposted path runs on the rocky hillside with ravishing views while it passes the ski lifts on the slopes of Mt Olympus.

Artemis was the goddess of hunting, natural environment and virginity. When she was born she helped her mother to deliver her twin brother Apollo, and became the protector of childbirth and labour.

From Troodos Square, the signposted Atalante Trail begins by an information board at the end of a boardwalk located by the playground next to the main road. The well-trodden path runs beneath pine trees on the hillside and soon passes the **Jubilee Hotel** on the right. Cross a dry streambed and continue to the left, and shortly after the path splits; the Atalante Trail is marked with an arrow and goes to the left, but keep to the right on the unmarked trail running slightly uphill. Walk along the stony path on the rocky slope with views to pine-covered mountains and soon the buildings of Troodos are visible on the left.

WALK 15 – ARTEMIS TRAIL

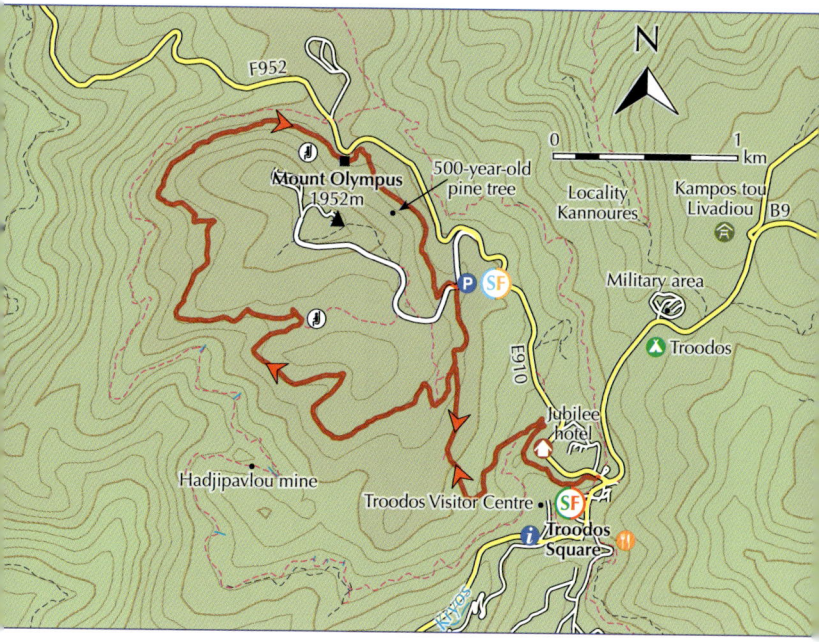

As the path bends right, join a track and keep right. About 45min from Troodos Square, after a gentle uphill section, at a junction you join the Artemis Trail. Keep left as the iron arrow indicates.

Alternative start/official Artemis Trail
In the car park on the F953 road there is an information board where the Artemis Trail officially starts. Take the path by the board and walk on the rocky hillside. A few minutes later reach a junction: keep straight on as the iron arrow indicates.

Main route continues
Walk on the mountainside beneath pine trees with views to the left. About 5min after the iron arrow at the junction, cross a forest track and continue on its other side. For the next 30–40min follow the path on the rocky mountainside through pine forest, often with stunning views to the left.

A narrow section of the Artemis Trail snakes between exposed rocks and steep drops

Pass a **ski lift** and as the path bends to the left you pass a building. Once again, follow the narrow path on the rocky mountainside with stunning views on your left. In the hazy distance the salt lake near Limassol, and then Prodromos village hugged by mountains in the valley, can be spotted. You'll see the peak of Mt Olympus with the radar dome as you walk through black pine forest.

The stony path runs on the sometimes barren mountainside with rocks towering on the right, and soon a snaking tarmac road comes into view.

An hour after passing the first ski slope, arrive at a green-roofed restaurant building and ski lifts. The path continues in-between the building and a lift, getting very close to the tarmac road. After the building, the path swings away from the road and runs slightly uphill.

Walk through pine forest and shortly arrive at a 500-year-old giant black **pine**. Carry straight on and very soon pass under another ski lift cable. Arrive at a forest track and a few metres later leave it to the left. Join the path and shortly afterwards reach a tarmac road with an information board which is the official start of the Artemis Trail – and the end of the walk for those using the alternative start/finish point.

If you started from Troodos Square, continue on the path by the information board. Walk on the rocky hillside and a few minutes later reach the junction where the trail from Troodos Square joins the Artemis Trail. Go left and retrace your steps to **Troodos Square**.

WALK 16
Caledonia circular

Start/finish	Psilo Dendro restaurant, Pano Platres (N34.89586, E32.86863)
Distance	9km
Total ascent/descent	420m
Grade	2
Time	2hr 30min–3hr
Refreshments	Restaurants in Platres, and Psilo Dendro at start of walk
Access	Psilo Dendro is located on the B8 road between Platres and Troodos. Parking available at restaurant.

This is a well-known and popular nature trail by the rushing Kryos river – one of the few rivers in Cyprus that carries water all year round. The best time to see the waterfall is probably during the spring months when the most water is cascading down. The clear and well-maintained shady path crosses the river mainly on bridges. The second part of the trail takes you across a pine-covered mountainside with impressive views along the way. The final section of the trail is the first section of Walk 17 (Pouziaris Trail) in reverse.

The nature trail starts by the information board at the restaurant car park. From here, walk straight up alongside the fence on a concrete road to the next information board. Follow the well-trodden, rocky footpath beneath trees and between huge rocks by the Kryos river, and soon reach the first bridge.

Walking between golden oaks, cross the rushing river several times on wooden bridges. After about half an hour, reach the **Caledonia Falls** where the ice-cold water comes crashing down from rocks at a height of 13m.

> The **Caledonia Falls** were named by Scots who visited the Platres area in 1878. They named the waterfall after their homeland: Caledonia was the Latin name for Scotland, given by the Romans.

Many people follow the river upstream only to the waterfall; however, the trail continues. After the waterfall continue on the path and ascend the steep steps. At the top of Caledonia Falls, go over another bridge and then continue slightly uphill. The path might be muddy and slippery here and you will have to cross

Walking in Cyprus

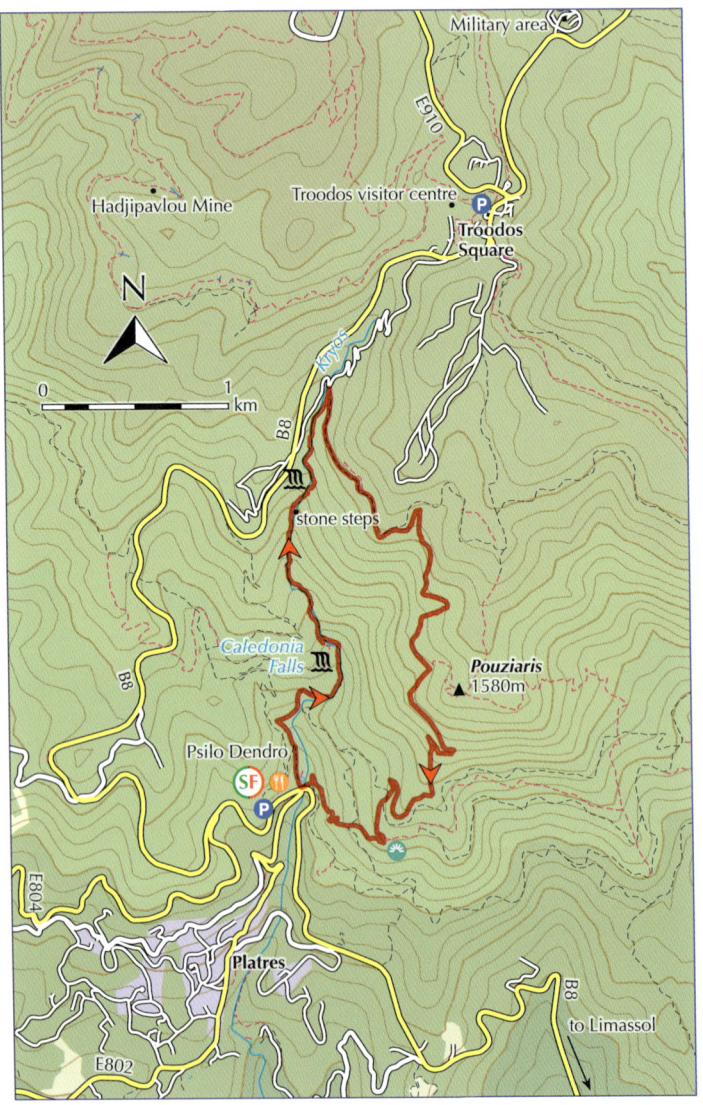

WALK 16 – CALEDONIA CIRCULAR

the river on rocks a few more times. The sound of rushing water accompanies you as you walk upstream amid the moss-covered rocks.

The path progresses steadily uphill, and about 30min after leaving Caledonia Falls you arrive at a set of very steep **stone steps** with railings. Just before the top of the steps there is a viewpoint where you can catch your breath and admire the water gushing down on rocks. Soon, nearing the old Troodos–Platres road, the water gently runs over and around smaller rocks.

Emerge onto a road by an information board. Go right on the track marked as 'Archbishop Makarious III

Caledonia waterfall

Trail'. Follow the forest track beneath pine trees for about 15min then leave it to the right on a narrow path as the sign indicates. As the path follows the contour of the mountainside, there are fewer pine trees and more fine views towards the south coast and the village of Platres down below.

The rocky path descends beneath kermes oaks (*Quercus coccifera*) and pines and occasionally gets very narrow and loose. About 40min after leaving the forest track there is a narrow path on the left. This path goes up to Pouziaris peak as part of Walk 17 (Pouziaris Trail). Continue straight on downhill: this part of the trail is the first section of the Pouziaris Trail from Psilo Dendro.

Walk on the mountainside with huge rocks towering on the left and stunning views on the right. You soon start to descend but this time the views are obstructed by trees. Reach a forest track and then continue on its other side slightly to the left. Soon, at a junction, bear right. A few minutes later there is a final opportunity to admire the views at a **viewpoint** from rocks.

About 10min after the previous one, cross another forest track and continue on its other side straight on downhill. Take a few steps and after a steep downhill section on loose surface zigzag back to **Psilo Dendro**.

WALK 17
Pouziaris Trail

Start/finish	Psilo Dendro restaurant, Pano Platres (N34.89586, E32.86863)
Distance	9km
Total ascent/descent	430m
Grade	2
Time	3hr
Refreshments	Restaurants in Platres, and Psilo Dendro at start of walk
Access	Psilo Dendro is located on the B8 road between Platres and Troodos. Parking available at restaurant.

The narrow, rocky path cut into the hillside climbs up to Pouziaris peak where memorable views welcome you. It then runs mainly downhill with more grand views along the way. Diverse scenery accompanies you during this pleasant walk on pine-covered slopes. The first hour of the walk is the final section of Walk 16 (Caledonia circular) in reverse.

Starting from the Psilo Dendro car park, keep left on the main road (B8). The trail begins a few metres away on the left, at the Pouziaris Trail information board. The path starts zigzagging steeply uphill through pine forest and about 10min later it reaches a track. Cross over the track and continue on its other side, straight uphill.

Soon reach a junction and keep left. (You will return to this junction from the path on the right.) Cross another forest track and continue on its other side, bearing left slightly. Ascend steadily beneath trees at first and then walk on the mountainside with rocks towering on the right and great views on the left.

About an hour after starting the trail, turn right uphill on a narrow, stony path and soon climb amid kermes oaks. The path going straight on is Walk 16 (Caledonia circular). The ground becomes less rough and it might be covered with dry pine needles as you climb among giant pines. Make the final ascent on a stony path to reach **Pouziaris peak** (1580m) 10–15min after the junction where you turned right.

Take a rest after your climb and enjoy the excellent scenery from the **summit of Pouziaris**. On a clear day, the panorama unfolds from the red roofs of the

WALK 17 – POUZIARIS TRAIL

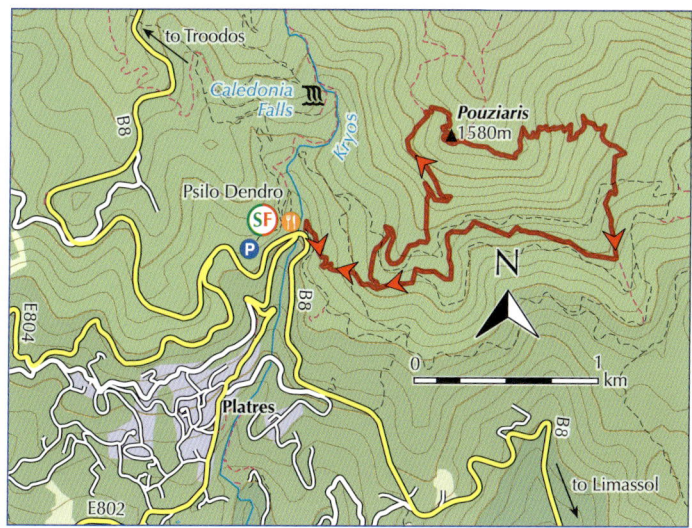

houses of Platres to the coastline, often bathed in hazy sunshine. Even the outline of Limassol can be spotted in the blurred distance.

Continue on the path, and at a junction go right and downhill as the 'Psilo Dendro (6.5km)' sign indicates. As the vegetation thins out, excellent views accompany you on the right, while a rocky mountainside dominates on the left. The path winds its way slightly uphill to a junction where you keep straight and then start to descend.

As you zigzag downhill the views are ever-changing, from the peak with two radar domes in front of you to the surrounding mountains, and towards the coast to the south. About 45min after leaving Pouziaris peak the path widens a bit and meets a disused, overgrown track from the right – but carry straight on as the sign indicates.

Descend steeply on an uneven rocky path and turn sharply right where indicated by a huge sign. Shortly, cross a forest track and continue straight downhill on its opposite side. Follow the curve of the mountain gently downhill; soon cross a dry streambed and then walk over huge rocks. The path then smoothes out and carries on downhill before running very gently uphill for about a kilometre.

After crossing two rockfalls the route starts to descend again. Emerge onto a forest track and continue on its other side downhill. At around 8km there are still

The most exposed section of the trail provides exceptional views

views towards Limassol and you arrive back at the junction with signs. Continue straight on downhill.

Soon cross a forest track and continue on its other side, straight downhill. Take a few steps down, and after a steep downhill section zigzag back to **Psilo Dendro**.

WALK 18
Loymata ton Aeton Trail

Start/finish	Amiantos playground (N34.92019, E32.93310)
Distance	4km
Total Ascent/descent	150m
Grade	1
Time	1hr 30min
Refreshments	Taverns in Amiantos village
Access	From the direction of Limassol, follow the B8 towards Troodos and take the E801 to Amiantos after the village of Trimiklini. Parking available at playground.

This short but spectacular walk starts from the edge of Amiantos village and initially follows a stream, which it crosses a few times before reaching a point where there is the opportunity to climb up to an EOKA hideout. The second part of the trail runs along hillside with some great views towards the river gorge.

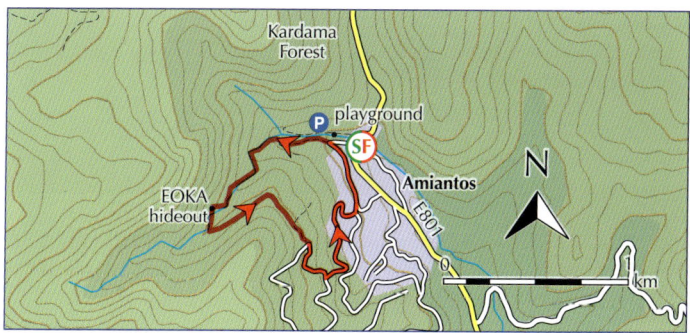

Follow the stony road leading uphill with the stream on your right and a few minutes later arrive at another dirt road where there are water tanks on the right. An information board (actually a blank wooden board without any information at the time of writing) marks the beginning of the path, which starts to the left between golden oaks.

Follow the stony path slightly uphill through the gorge with the stream on your right. Soon cross the stream over rocks and then continue slightly uphill with a rocky mountainside towering on your right.

The outward route from Amiantos follows a stream

Occasional painted red arrows indicate the way. Pass by boulders and soon cross the stream again. Continue between myrtle (*Myrtus communis*) and golden oaks and shortly reach a sign: 'hideout'. On the right, a narrow, steep path with worn steps leads up to a small **EOKA hideout**. EOKA fighters used these hideouts in the mountains between 1955 and 1959. Climb up to the hideout and then descend back to the path, which continues through the gorge.

Soon cross the stream again and walk alongside the gurgling water. All too soon the path bends to the left and leaves the stream. A painted red arrow marks the turn; the path seems to continue straight on for a bit as well, but there is a line of stones 'closing' it, indicating that you shouldn't go that way.

There are some stone steps as you climb between pines and golden oaks, and soon a view to the gorge on your left. Then the path swings away from the gorge and starts to descend.

When you reach a dirt track, go straight uphill as the painted red arrow indicates and a few minutes later arrive at a junction. Go downhill, slightly left, and a few minutes later reach a tarmac road. Go left, and shortly reach another tarmac road. Keep left again and carry straight on all the way back to the **playground**.

WALK 19
Madari Trail

Start/finish	Locality Doxa Soi o Theos information board (N34.95593, E32.96294)
Distance	13km; including Teisia tis Madaris extension: 16.5km
Total ascent/descent	690m; including extension: 825m
Grade	3
Time	5hr; including extension: 6hr
Refreshments	None
Access	Arriving from the direction of Karvounas village on the E909 road, turn left onto the F944 road just before Kyperounta village. Pass the 'Adventure Mountain Park' and there is a parking area on the left-hand side of the road, opposite the Locality Doxa Soi o Theos information board.

The well-trodden path goes initially steeply uphill and then there are some gentle undulating sections as you head towards the Madari fire lookout station. Enjoy the splendid 360-degree panorama from a viewpoint. The trail can then be extended with the short Teisia tis Madaris Trail, from where you can observe an impressive example of a sheeted dike complex. From the fire lookout station the trail runs mainly downhill and from Locality Selladi tou Karamanli it is part of the E4 long-distance trail.

Follow the path that starts by the information board and then zigzags steeply uphill between golden oaks, rock roses and pines. Almost immediately you have some views to the left, but this is just a taster as even better views await you during the walk. The path climbs steadily uphill and about 15min after leaving Locality Doxa Soi o Theos you have the first views to the right towards the Troodos. The path bends gently left and soon allows fine views to the Madari (Adelfoi) peak in the distance.

There is a small building at the top of Madari, which is one of the 13 **fire lookout stations** located on some of the highest peaks of Cyprus. From May to October, when the risk of fire is high, these lookouts are manned around the clock. The fire-watcher is familiar with the area, as he usually comes from a local village, and can locate the fire and guide the firemen accurately.

WALKING IN CYPRUS

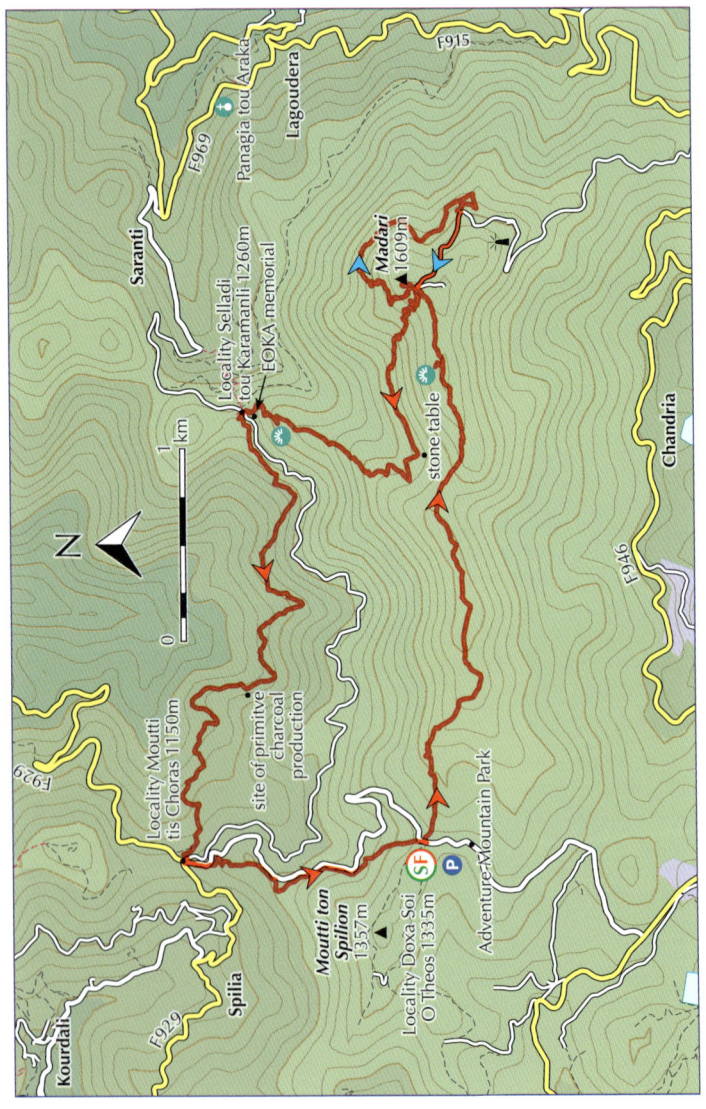

Continue on the sometimes narrow path with views to the cultivated slopes of Kyperounta village on the right-hand side. An hour into the walk you'll notice a narrow path on the left; it is a short detour to the mountain top with a bench and trigpoint where you can enjoy a magnificent 360-degree panorama. The Kyrenia mountain range, Morfou Bay and the north coast are easily visible on a clear day. Drink in the view, return to the path and continue along the ridge.

About 10min later arrive at a junction with an information board near the fire lookout station. At this junction you have several choices: as well as continuing on the main route, you can walk up a steep, concrete path to the fire lookout building from where there are views towards the mountains and Nicosia, the Kyrenia mountain range and the recognisable radar dome on the peak of Kionia. There is also an option to extend your walk on the 3.5km-long Teisia tis Madaris Trail.

Extension: Teisia tis Madaris Trail

The signposted Teisia tis Madaris Trail starts from the information board which describes some of the geological characteristics, such as sheeted dikes, that can be observed in this area.

At first the narrow path curves steeply downhill on the rocky mountainside, which soon becomes rich with vegetation. On this circular route overgrown nature labels describe various plants. You can make a detour to a viewpoint with a bench not long after the start of the trail, but the path continues downhill, often with great views to the left and with huge rocks towering on the right-hand side.

The views change on your left as the path curves around the **Madari peak**. There is a tiny village down below, and then from a viewpoint you might be able to spot the roof of the Panagia tou Araka church in Lagoudera. Continue, taking in the mountain views on your left. There is a gentle uphill section and then just after the 2km mark the path splits; go right uphill (the other path leads towards the antennas) and a few minutes later emerge onto a dirt road. Turn right and walk back to the junction near the fire lookout station.

Main route continues

To continue on the main route, from the junction, follow the path downhill marked 'Selladi Karamanli'. Pines and golden oaks are the main vegetation as you zigzag downhill with views to the right. Like a grey river dashing down the mountainside, deposits of talus rock (rocky debris) cross the path, and in springtime pink rock roses give a dash of bright colour. As you descend, enjoy the fantastic views on the right-hand side.

About half an hour after leaving the junction near the fire lookout station, reach a **stone table** with stools in the shade of pines next to the path. As the path bends right you can glimpse the fire lookout building on the peak of Madari in the distance on the right. About 50–60min after starting the descent from the fire lookout station, notice a wooden arrow with a sign in Greek pointing to a path by a bench. This takes you to a **viewpoint**. From the wooden sign, continue downhill and 10min later arrive at **Locality Selladi tou Karamanli** (1260m). There is an EOKA monument close to the map board.

Emerge to a tarmac lane, the trail continues downhill on its other side, by the Moutti tis Choras sign. It is also marked with 'E4' as it is a section of the long-distance trail. Walk downhill; the hillside is scattered with moss-covered rocks beneath golden oaks. Soon, the trail takes you across two deposits of talus rock.

The villages of Agia Eirini and Kannavia nestle in a valley on your right. Pass a **site of primitive charcoal production**, then the path widens a bit and soon joins a forest track. Go right as the E4 sign indicates and a few minutes later arrive at another forest track. The path continues on the other side of this track, a few metres uphill to the left. Shortly emerge onto a tarmac road and on its other side there is an information board. Arrive at **Locality Moutti tis Choras** about an hour after leaving Locality Selladi tou Karamanli.

Follow the 'Doxa Soi o Theos 1.8km' sign. Take the road signposted 'E4' towards Kyperounta and about 50m later leave the tarmac road to the right as the sign indicates. Follow the path marked 'E4', between the dirt track and the tarmac road. The path runs mainly parallel to the tarmac road with some views between the tree crowns to the mountains. On the right is Spilia village, with the fire lookout station on Madari to the left in the distance. Continue steadily uphill and about 30min after Locality Moutti tis Choras emerge onto a tarmac road, turn right and a few metres later arrive back at **Locality Doxa Soi o Theos**.

Benches are located on some of the best viewing spots along the way

WALK 20
Kannavia circular

Start/finish	Kannavia village, at the junction of the F929 road and Andrea Patsalidi Street (N34.98073, E32.97637)
Distance	19km
Total ascent/descent	830m
Grade	3
Time	5hr 30min–6hr (+ allow minimum 1hr to explore the EOKA headquarters)
Refreshments	Water may be found at Locality Straorouthkias but take plenty with you
Access	Kannavia is located on the F929 road, 10km from the B9. There is roadside parking in the village.

This long walk connects three nature trails and a section of the E4, and at times also follows dirt tracks. The first 3km is a strenuous climb with outstanding views. Along the way, take time to enjoy a peaceful, hidden viewpoint where you can hear birdsong and admire the grand mountains. There is an opportunity to visit the EOKA headquarters on the hill above Spilia before descending to Agia Eirini. The final short section of the walk follows a tarmac road connecting Agia Eirini with Kannavia village.

The trail starts from the information board on Andrea Patsalidi Street in Kannavia. Go downhill and a few metres later reach 28th Oktourion Street, where the 'Selladi tou Karamanli' sign with an arrow indicates the direction.

Walk along the wide track with a valley on your left for about 600m, then a path – marked 'Selladi tou Karamanli' – starts to the left. Go downhill on this narrow path and almost immediately cross over a small **bridge** and continue uphill on the other side. There are some wooden steps by a small cultivated piece of land on the slope but soon you climb between golden oaks and pines.

Cross a rocky streambed, and as the path climbs higher from the valley, rock roses appear between the pines and golden oaks. Zigzag steeply uphill on the narrow path for about an hour with rewarding views to the pine-covered mountains and the valley. There are great views to Agia Eirini and Kannavia villages as well as to the Madari peak.

WALK 20 – KANNAVIA CIRCULAR

The views open up to lush, forested mountainsides

After an hour of strenuous climbing from Kannavia, arrive at a road. The 'Selladi tou Karamanli' sign with an arrow suggests walking on the road, but you can get to Selladi tou Karamanli along a narrow and picturesque path which starts on the right.

Walk slightly downhill between golden oaks and pines and as the path swings around the mountain you can enjoy the views. Like tiny model houses on a giant plotting board, the buildings of Agia Eirini and Kannavia nestle in the valley. About 15min from the tarmac road, arrive at **Locality Pezounokremos** where

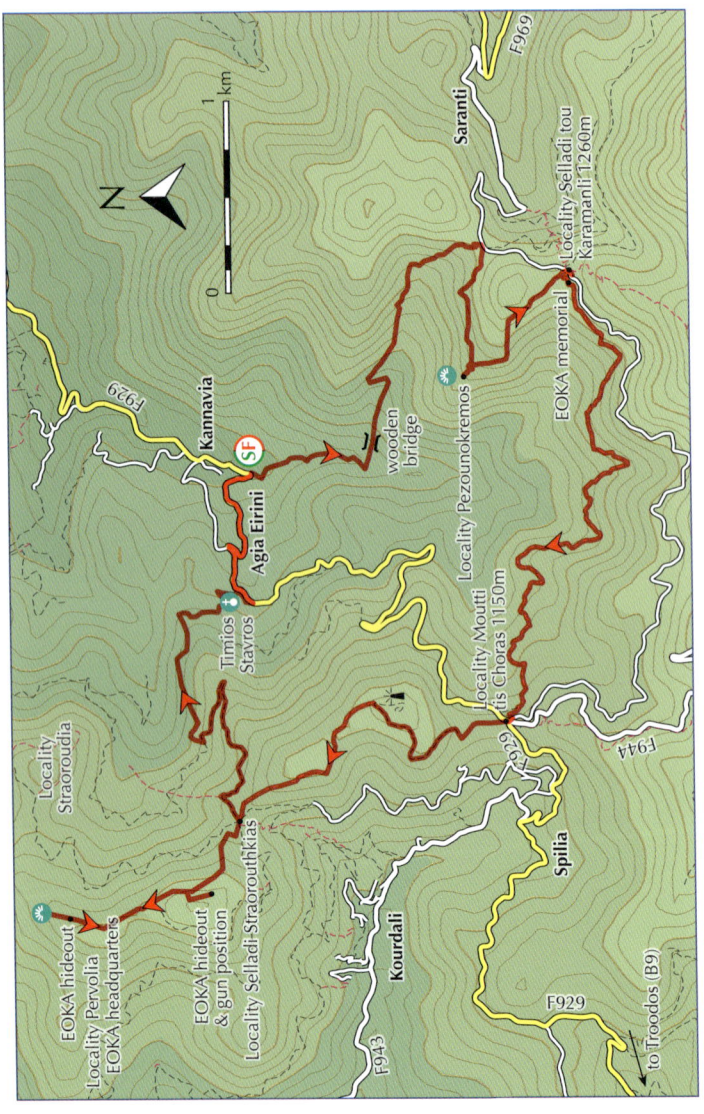

a sign indicates a viewpoint 130m away. If you make the detour to this roofed viewpoint you will be rewarded with a 180-degree panorama of the mountains and the valley.

From the viewpoint, retrace your steps to Locality Pezounokremos and continue to the right. Follow the less-used, stony path curving around the edge of the mountainside, going slightly uphill for about 30min to arrive at **Locality Selladi tou Karamanli**. There is an **EOKA monument** on the hillside, to the right of an information board.

EOKA

Former armoury near the EOKA headquarters

EOKA (Ethniki Organosi tou Kyprakou Agona – National Organisation of Cypriot Fighters) was founded in 1955 and its main aim was to end the British rule and achieve enosis (union) with Greece. The founder and leader of the organisation was Georgios Grivas, who managed the first EOKA operations from Nicosia/Lefkoşa but then joined his team in the Troodos mountains. The second-in-command of the organisation was Grigoris Afxentiou. Between 1955 and 1959 EOKA targeted the British, and 371 British servicemen lost their lives.

EOKA didn't achieve enosis but the independent Republic of Cyprus was born in 1960.

As a walker you can see numerous hideouts in the mountains, as well as monuments in villages, as the young men who lost their lives as EOKA fighters are remembered as heroes by Greek Cypriots.

Map of the hideouts

Continue sharply to the right towards 'Moutti tis Choras (3.8km)'. As you walk between golden oaks, the slope is scattered with moss-covered rocks. The path winds steadily downhill with views to the right, and about 45min from Selladi tou Karamanli it widens a bit and soon joins a forest track. Keep right and a few minutes later join another forest track. The path, marked 'E4', continues a few metres further uphill to the left.

Emerge onto a tarmac road at a junction with the **Locality Moutti tis Choras** information board. From this junction take the unmarked dirt road on the right. Shortly, when the dirt track splits, keep right. On the left a group of red roofs, the houses of Spilia, break through the greenery of the hills, and as you continue slightly uphill you can enjoy views towards Morfou Bay as well.

When the track splits again, go left (the right track goes up to a radio antenna). From Locality Moutti tis Choras the dirt track curves around the mountainside for 2.5km and arrives at **Locality Selladi Straorouthkias** at a seven-way junction.

There is a map board, fountain and picnic area here. As you arrive at the junction, you'll take the first track on the right to continue to Agia Eirini. (From this junction it's about 1hr, mostly downhill, back to Kannavia.) However, before you go down to the village you can visit the hideouts on the hill: take the trail marked 'Hideouts' and zigzag uphill for about 15min.

On the hillside you'll see **hideouts**, **heavy gun positions**, the **EOKA headquarters** and lookouts. Everything is signposted and you can discover the hillside and its history. Follow the 'Headquarters' sign to arrive at the map of the hideouts with a flag mast. From here, follow the 'Hideout No.3' sign to reach to a **viewpoint** where you can enjoy the fantastic panorama of Morfou Bay.

THE BATTLE OF SPILIA

On 12 December 1955, the British Army attempted to encircle the headquarters of EOKA on the hill near Spilia. The units of Georgios Grivas and Grigoris Afxentiou fought the ascending British troops on the north and south sides of the mountain. There was thick fog on the mountain and the EOKA units managed to escape towards the west. When the British troops reached the summit from opposing sides they couldn't see anything in the fog; thinking they were surrounded by EOKA fighters, they started to shoot each other. The incident led to the highest number of casualties caused by friendly fire during this war.

Retrace your steps to the seven-way junction and continue on the dirt track marked 'To Agia Eirini'. The track swings around the hillside and soon joins another track. Go left downhill. A path signposted 'Agia Eirini' starts from the dirt road on the right. A few stone steps lead downhill between pines, then the path curves around the mountainside with views to the valley and the pine-covered slopes and soon arrives at another dirt track. Go right towards Agia Eirini.

Walk past some cultivated land and then leave the dirt track and continue on a path on the left. Zigzag downhill to **Timios Stavros church** and then continue to the left and meet a tarmac road at **Agia Eirini**. Go right, downhill, and arrive at a junction. Go left, and soon leave Agia Eirini. About 10min later arrive back at **Kannavia** where the walk started.

WALK 21
Asinou Trail

Start/finish	Cemetery near Agios Theodoros in Solea Valley (N35.04465, E32.92945)
Distance	10km
Total ascent/descent	375m
Grade	2
Time	4hr
Refreshments	Water at Asinou church and restaurants nearby
Access	On the B9 road from the direction of Kakopetria, turn towards Agios Theodoros on the F975 road. Follow the narrow road through the village and look for an information board on the left. Turn left onto the narrow concrete road by the information board; a few minutes later this reaches a cemetery where there are plenty of places to park.

From the edge of Agios Theodoros village, a narrow path takes you along wooded hillsides to the UNESCO World Heritage-listed 12th-century Asinou church. The barn church is located 3km from Nikitari village and is home to some of the finest Byzantine frescos of the 12th to 17th centuries. This out-and-back trail is well signposted, easy to follow and offers some splendid views towards a bay and the forested mountains.

From the cemetery, the road becomes a dirt road and a few minutes later it splits. Keep left and walk uphill between old almond trees. The landscape before you is dominated by pine-covered mountains.

Shortly leave the dirt track to the left on a path marked 'Palospova alt 520m'. Wooden steps lead up to a narrow path beneath pines. Follow the path along the hillside with great views towards Morfou Bay. About 20–30min after joining the path, reach a dirt track. Go left downhill as indicated by an arrow and a few metres later leave it to the right on a footpath marked 'Asinou 3.6km'.

Continue on the pine-covered hillside and shortly reach **Selladi Zevxis** (altitude 652m) where you can enjoy the panorama of the bay and its surroundings. From here, go downhill on the path, ignoring a track. About 10min after Selladi Zevxis, emerge onto a dirt track and then continue on its other side as indicated

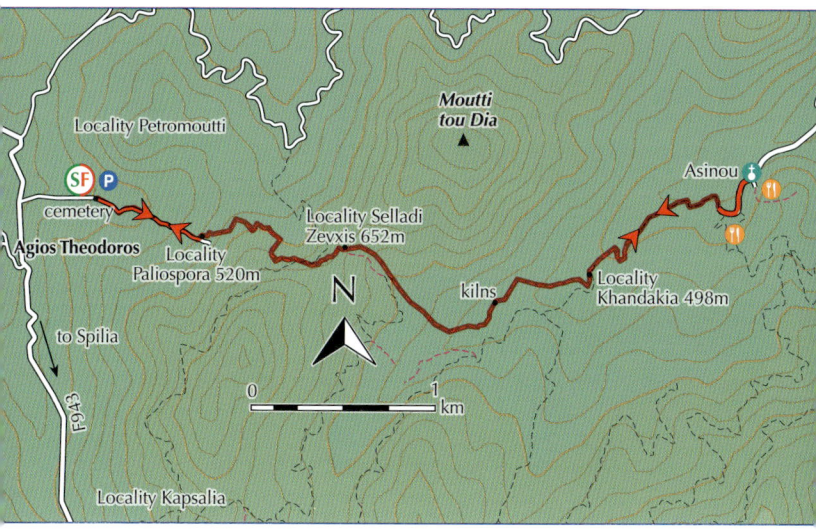

by the 'Asinou 2.9km' sign. The path is a bit wider here and the view in front of you is dominated by a towering mountain.

Keep right at the next junction as the sign indicates, and a few metres downhill reach a dirt track. Keep left as the 'Asinou 2.3km' sign indicates. Ignore the track on the left and shortly pass two **kilns** with an information board. Continue on the narrow path with a streambed on your right.

> Pine tar was at one time used in pharmaceutics and industry in Cyprus. In the island's forests you'll see many abandoned stone **kilns** which were used to produce tar. Two pits were made – one larger and higher and connected to a smaller pit by a channel. Small pieces of wood were layered vertically to fill the bigger pit. It was then covered with mud, moss and ferns and lit from the top through a small opening. As the wood burned, the liquid raw tar flowed from the large pit into the small pit. The tar was then put into smaller wooden moulds/containers.

Pass a water tank and go over a bridge, then turn left at a dirt road. Very soon reach an information board (**Khandakia**, 498m). Bear left on the dirt road; the road becomes tarmac by some buildings and leads to **Asinou church**. There are some restaurants near the church.

Tar kilns

The 12th-century **Asinou church** is home to some of the finest Byzantine frescos. The entire interior of the church is covered with these colourful artworks, which date from the 12th to the 17th century. The building is a UNESCO World Heritage Site.

After visiting the church, retrace your steps back to the **cemetery** near Agios Theodoros.

The beautiful Asinou church

WALK 22
Panagia tou Araka – Stavros tou Agiasmati

Start/finish	Panagia tou Araka, Lagoudera (N34.96502, E33.00713)
Distance	15km
Total ascent/descent	700m
Grade	2
Time	5hr
Refreshments	Water available by Stavros tou Agiasmati church; shop in Lagoudera
Access	From Karvounas on the B9, take the E909 towards Kyperounta and then follow signs to Lagoudera, which is on the F915.

This section of the E4 runs as a nature trail connecting two Byzantine churches, both listed as World Heritage Sites. It is a linear walk in the CTO (Cyprus Tourism Organisation) Nature Trail booklet, but as Stavros tou Agiasmati stands remotely at the end of the trail, you will most probably have to retrace your steps to Lagoudera.

From Lagoudera, you first walk alongside vineyards and almond trees, then the narrow path runs on a forested mountainside with magnificent views.

Stavros tou Agiasmati is closed but you can pre-arrange a visit. Ask for the contact number at one of the CTO offices (see Appendix A).

PANAGIA TOU ARAKA CHURCH

The UNESCO-listed 12th-century church is located just outside of Lagoudera. The name derives from the Greek word *arakas*, or *arakiotissa*, which means wild pea. The church is home to Cyprus' most complete series of frescos from the Middle Byzantine period.

In the 14th century the roof was covered with a protective timber roof. As is typical of the churches in the Troodos, a separate wooden roof covers the dome.

From Panagia tou Araka church, walk up the tarmac road to the village of **Lagoudera**. At the junction, go left towards Lefkosia. At the next intersection, carry

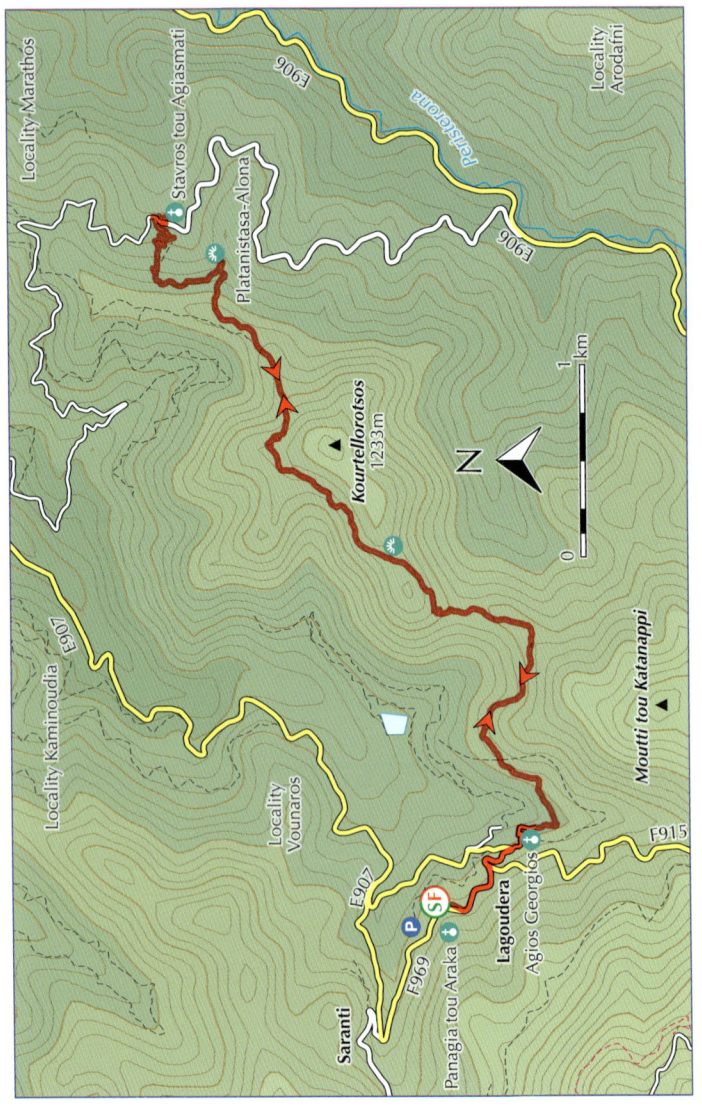

WALK 22 – PANAGIA TOU ARAKA – STAVROS TOU AGIASMATI

Panagia tou Araka church

straight on. (There is an E4 sign on a lamppost.) At the next junction keep left downhill, and shortly after that go right. Follow the nature trail sign straight on and a few minutes later pass Lagoudera's final house. Go downhill and soon cross a streambed. Pass by huge rocks and then the path crawls slightly uphill alongside vineyards and almond trees.

About 10–15min after passing the final house, cross a dirt track and continue uphill on its other side. On the left the view is dominated by the houses of Lagoudera nestled on the steep hillside with the peak of Madari towering above them. Soon, rock roses and golden oaks replace the old vineyards and almond trees and a reservoir down below can be spotted. The stony path continues steadily uphill with magnificent views of the surrounding mountains, and about 20min after the first it meets another dirt track. Keep left and a few metres further on leave the dirt track to the left as the E4 sign indicates.

Pine trees are the main vegetation and mountains dominate the views as you walk along the stony path. Approximately halfway along the route you reach a **viewpoint** where the splendid vista of Cape Kormakitis and Morfou Bay greets you. From this point, continue to walk mainly downhill for 40–50min to reach the next signposted viewpoint (**Platanistasa-Alona**). This part of the route is made more difficult by very steep downhill sections on occasionally loose surfaces. The narrow path runs beneath pine trees and from the Platanistasa-Alona viewpoint it bends to the left and soon runs between almond trees.

The path splits and a wooden sign shows the two different routes: the steeper one is only 160m, while the other gently descends for 310m. Take either branch as the two paths soon rejoin just before emerging onto a dirt track. Keep left and then reach a junction where you go right and walk down to the **church**. There is a picnic table in the shade of trees, and running water and toilets can be found by the church.

The 15th-century UNESCO-listed church of **Stavros tou Agiasmati** remains slightly remote as it is situated 3km outside of Platanistasa village. It is home to the most complete 15th-century mural paintings in Cyprus. The church is closed but there is a phone number on the door to call if you haven't pre-arranged a visit and you want to see the interior.

After visiting the church, take a rest under the shade of trees and then retrace your steps to **Lagoudera**.

The trail offers unrestricted views to the surrounding area

WALK 23
Politiko Nature Trail

Start/finish	1km NE of Machairas Monastery (N34.94416, E33.19524)
Distance	There and back: 12km; circular: 8.5km
Total ascent/descent	There and back: 330m/330m; circular: 330m/330m
Grade	2
Time	There and back: 4hr; circular: 2hr 30min
Refreshments	Machairas Monastery
Access	On the E902 road, turn right just before Machairas Monastery, and about 1km downhill a map board marks the beginning of the trail; there is space to park here.

This nature trail follows a quiet valley cut by the Pedieos river. The mighty building of the Machairas Monastery overlooks the valley as you start the trail. The path then undulates on the hillside following the lush riverbed. Like many other nature trails in this area, Politiko Nature Trail ends abruptly by a rural road, therefore you will need to retrace your steps.

There is an option to make this route circular by returning to the starting point via tracks.

MACHAIRAS MONASTERY

An icon of the Virgin Mary – believed to be painted by the Apostle Luke – was found in a local cave in 1145 by two hermits, Neophytos and Ignatius, who used a knife to cut through thick bushes to reach it. A church was founded on the site in 1172 and was later expanded into a monastery. The name 'Machairas' comes from the Greek word *makhaira*, which means knife. In 1530 and then in 1892, fire destroyed the monastery but the icon survived.

From the information board, walk downhill on the dirt track and a few minutes later, where the road bends right, join a narrow path which starts on the right, going slightly uphill. The Pedieos riverbed splits the hills and the only building, a small church, can be spotted on the opposite side of the gorge. About 10min from the information board there is a small path leaving the trail to the right; it is a detour to an **EOKA hideout**.

WALKING IN CYPRUS

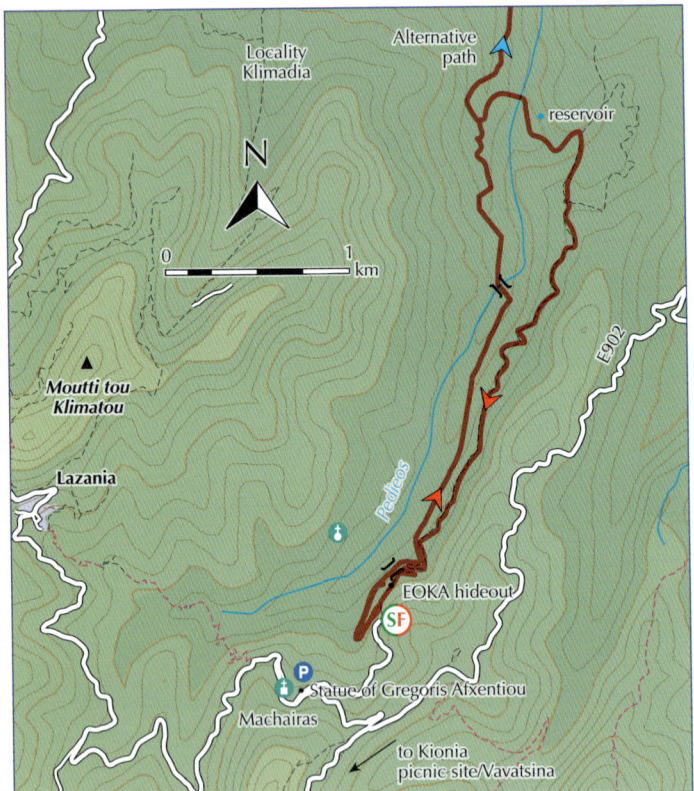

During EOKA's fights in the 1950s, **Grigoris Afxentiou**, their second-in-command, went into hiding in the Machairas Monastery. He was trapped and killed by the British in a hideout nearby on 3 March 1957. You can take a short detour to the hideout, which is decorated with wreaths. Afxentiou is regarded by the Cypriots as a national hero and a statue of him stands on the mountain close to the monastery, clearly visible from the Politiko Nature Trail.

However, the trail continues straight on and soon crosses a wooden **bridge**. There is an olive tree plantation down in the valley next to the river, but soon pine trees, golden oaks and rock roses are the main vegetation.

The nature trail follows the valley of the Pedieos stream

The narrow path meanders among pine trees. Keep straight on when the sign indicates and ignore any paths joining in from the right. As the valley narrows you can see the stony riverbed, and about 45min from the start you descend slightly to reach another wooden **bridge**. Cross over it and then continue on the other side of the valley with captivating views to the narrow gorge and the surrounding hills.

At 3km into the walk look out for a narrow path on the right. (Here you have the option to continue straight on to the end of the gorge and then retrace your steps, or you can make the route circular by taking the path on the right.)

Circular option

Take the narrow path on the right. Descend to the stream and cross over rocks. Climb up on the other side of the stream and reach a track. Go right and shortly pass a reservoir. At the track junction keep right uphill. This is a short but steep climb with some great views towards the nearby hills. At the big track junction take the second track from the right and head towards Kionia peak. Soon you can also see the monastery building in the distance. Ignore a path on the right and pass a map board and continue on the track. Pass the access path to the Eoka hideout and arrive back at the starting point just over an hour after you joined the track.

Crossing the Pedieos river

There and back option
Continue straight on the well trodden path.

A rocky slope with pines on the top dominates the views on the right. The path curves around the mountainside and as the gorge widens again you'll see a dirt track and then some cultivated fields on the slopes on the other side of the valley. The path runs downhill and crosses a stream, then you walk uphill and swing away from the valley. Notice some buildings on the hill to the left and arrive at a dirt track by a fence. Follow this track by cultivated lands and a few minutes later arrive at a tarmac road and map board, where the nature trail ends abruptly.

There is not much to see from this point, so retrace your steps on the charming path back to the information board marking the beginning of the trail.

WALK 24
Machairas Monastery – Fikardou

Start	Machairas Monastery (N34.94158, E33.18909)
Alternative start	Kionia picnic site (N34.92091, E33.19771)
Finish	Fikardou
Distance	5km; from Kionia picnic site: 10km
Total ascent/descent	310m/280m; from Kionia picnic site: 415m/745m
Grade	2
Time	2hr; from Kionia picnic site: 3hr 45min
Refreshments	Machairas Monastery, tavern in Lazania and restaurant in Fikardou
Access	From the A1 take the E105 towards Vavatsinia. Kionia picnic site (alternative start) is located about 8km north of Vavatsinia. For Machairas Monastery follow the road signs north from Kionia picnic site. Parking available at both.
Note	Starting from the Kionia picnic site adds an additional 1hr 45min (5km) to the walk. If you are planning to retrace your steps from Fikardou, allow plenty of time as there are some steep ascents along the way. Otherwise, transport from Fikardou should be arranged before the walk is started.

An E4-signed narrow path with excellent views to the mountains steeply descends from Machairas Monastery to a valley and then climbs to the tiny village of Lazania before continuing to the charming Fikardou village. Exploring the narrow streets of Fikardou feels like walking in the 18th century.

Starting from Kionia picnic site

Go up the steps between the picnic tables and arrive at the tarmac road that runs above the picnic site and leads up to the peak of Kionia with its radar dome. Turn right onto this road and follow it for about 600m to reach a **barrier**. An E4 sign with a map board on the right marks the start of the trail.

Leave the tarmac road to the right and walk uphill through a wooded area. The path passes the peak of Kionia with its dome towering at the top. Soon it gradually bends to the north and you walk along the ridge towards Machairas Monastery.

About 40min after leaving Kionia picnic site, start to zigzag downhill on the narrow stony path with views to pine-covered mountains as well as the snaking tarmac road below. Zigzag for 20–30min and emerge onto a dirt track. Keep right, and where another track joins in keep right again. About 10–15min after joining the dirt track you will reach a tarmac road junction; follow the tarmac road on the left towards **Machairas Monastery**, which you may opt to visit. From its car park continue on the tarmac road towards Lazania.

Inner gate of Machairas Monastery

Start from Machairas Monastery

From the monastery car park, walk on the tarmac road towards Lazania. The path starts on the right, going steeply downhill from the road about 200m from the car park. (At the time of writing the E4 sign was missing but the narrow path was clearly visible.) Lazania's houses clinging to the opposite hillside draw your attention as you walk downhill between shrubs for about 15min and arrive at a streambed at the bottom of the valley.

Cross the stream over rocks and continue slightly uphill. Soon descend again by another streambed fringed by plane trees. The stony path levels out and runs along the edge of the mountainside, and shortly after the first it crosses a second streambed. Continue on the other side, zigzagging uphill between rock roses, occasional pines and olive trees. The vegetation is never too thick and you always have views of the mountains around you. On the left is the peak of Kionia in the distance.

Walk alongside a stone retaining wall and cultivated area and pass by two concrete **water tanks**. Continue to ascend and shortly arrive at a track. Keep left and a few metres further on an E4 sign marks the way uphill on a path to the right. There are some old olive trees by the path on your left and in front you Lazania's houses dominate the slope.

WALK 24 – MACHAIRAS MONASTERY – FIKARDOU

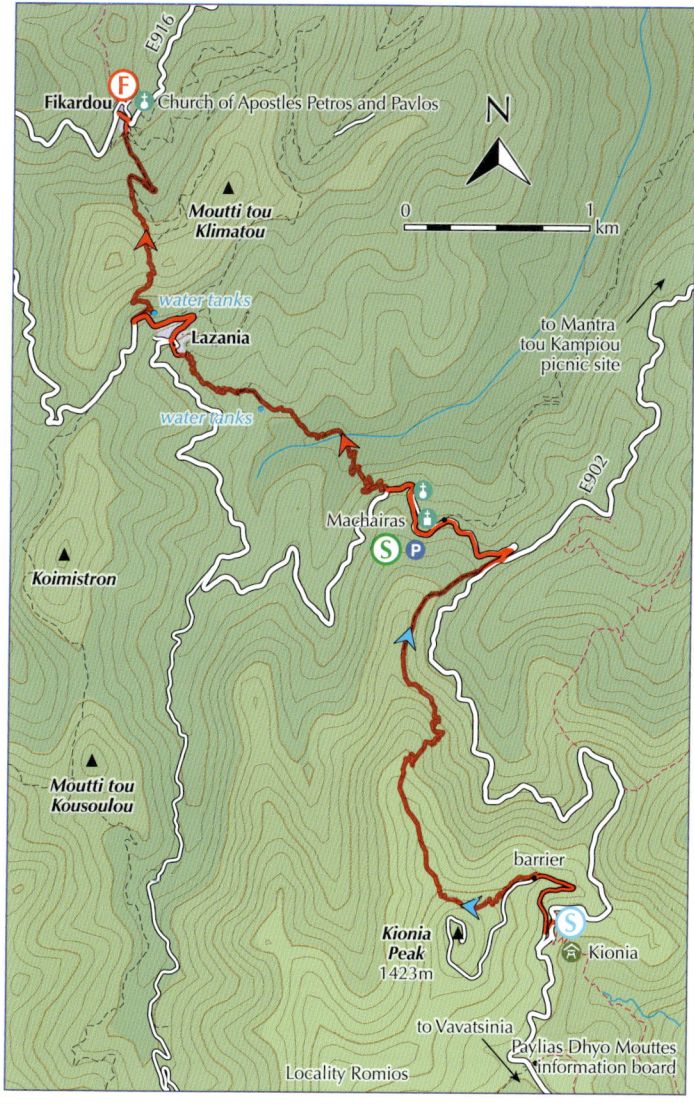

The narrow path goes through a shallow valley with sparse vegetation

When you reach a dirt track, go right and it soon becomes a path again. Zigzag uphill and arrive at a road. Go left as the E4 sign shows and arrive in **Lazania** about an hour after leaving the monastery. Follow a narrow street between the old village houses and at the end of this narrow street turn right. Soon pass a small restaurant, and follow the tarmac road as the E4 sign indicates.

After leaving the village, ignore the first access road to the right. Leave the tarmac road on the second access road to the right, about 200m from Lazania's last house. Go uphill on the stony track and just before reaching two water tanks, go left on a narrow path. Walk initially alongside a stone retaining wall with views to the roofs of Lazania's houses and the surrounding mountains.

Zigzag uphill between small shrubs and about 20min after leaving the tarmac road you will reach a gap between two hilltops. Start to descend towards Fikardou village with views towards the Kyrenia range and Morfou Bay. Pass a small house and a vineyard on the slope and continue to descend between golden oaks and other shrubs.

After a very steep downhill section you reach a concrete track; go left downhill. Soon it becomes a dirt track and as it swings around the mountainside the noises from the village can be heard. Arrive at a junction, keep right and walk into the village. Arrive in **Fikardou** about an hour after leaving Lazania.

> **Fikardou** is a tiny picturesque village with narrow streets. Some houses have been restored to give insight into 18th-century village life. Two of the houses have been turned into a small museum. The village received the Europa Nostra Award in 1987 for its efforts in heritage conservation.

From Fikardou, if you haven't done so already, you may be able to arrange a taxi back to your start point. There are also a couple of daily buses to Nicosia. Alternatively, you could retrace your steps, making a long and challenging day.

WALK 25
Kionia Nature Trail

Start/finish	Kionia picnic site (N34.92091, E33.19771)
Distance	15km
Total ascent/descent	690m
Grade	3
Time	4hr
Refreshments	Fountain at Kionia picnic site
Access	From the A1 take the E105 road towards Vavatsinia. Kionia picnic site is located about 8km from Vavatsinia. You can park at the picnic site.

The disused Profitis Elias Monastery and the Kionia picnic site are connected by the Kionia Nature Trail, which runs as part of the E4 long-distance trail. Impressive views of unspoilt mountains as well as towards Nicosia and the north accompany you during this walk.

From the road take the E4 path downhill, which takes you beneath the picnic site. Before long follow the narrow path on the hillside with a ravine on your left and with fine views to the nearby mountains. About 1km into the walk, ignore a narrow path on the right and within a few minutes, pass **Locality Platanouthkia** and

The narrow stony path follows a small gorge for a while

WALKING IN CYPRUS

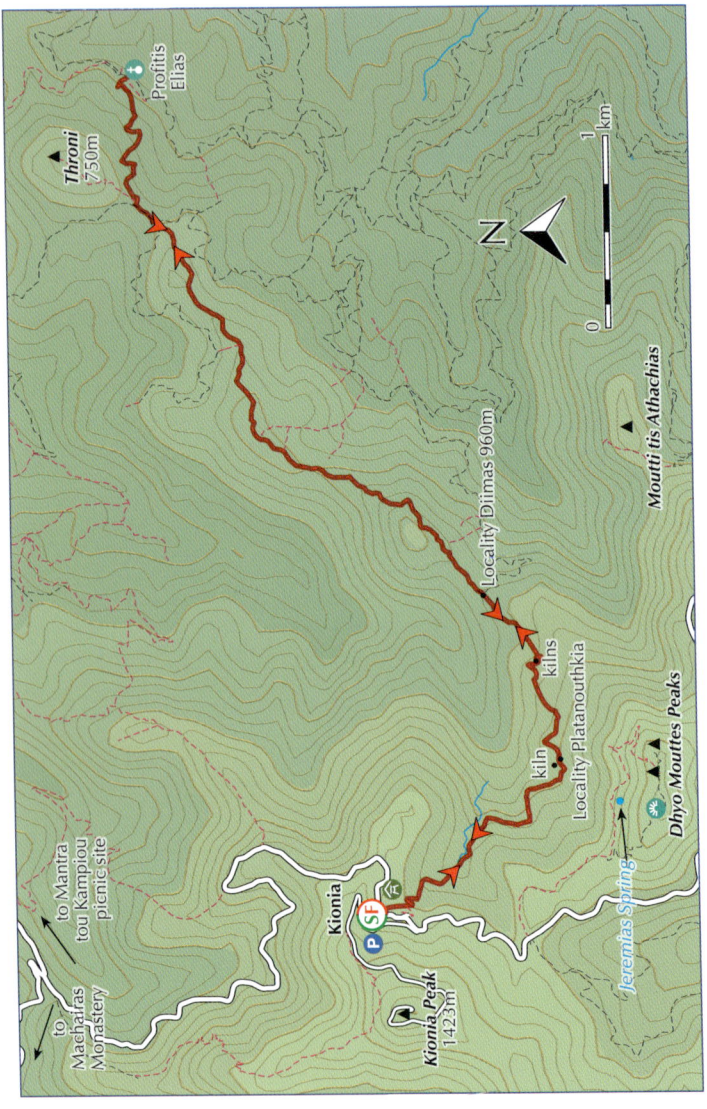

WALK 25 – KIONIA NATURE TRAIL

A beautiful view of the rolling hills just before descending to Profitis Elias church

the site of a **kiln**. Follow the path downhill beneath pine trees and golden oaks, and just before reaching a dirt track pass by two big tar production **kilns**.

Reach a dirt road (**Locality Diimas**, 960m) and keep left towards Profitis Elias. Soon walk along a ridge and as the path follows the contour of the mountain the view opens up towards Nicosia. Descend steadily and about 45min after the dirt road arrive at another dirt track and go left (there a sign indicates that Profitis Elias is 1km away).

Turn right off the road and continue downhill on the narrow path, which takes you to Profitis Elias picnic site (700m) and the abandoned **monastery**.

From Profitis Elias retrace your steps to **Kionia picnic site**. This will take about 2hr.

WALK 26
Kakokefalos – Mantra tou Kampiou Trail

Start/finish	Picnic bench at the bend in road 500m north of Kionia picnic site (N34.921599, E33.201086)
Distance	12.5km
Total ascent/descent	790m
Grade	2
Time	4hr
Refreshments	Water fountain at Mantra tou Kampiou picnic site
Access	From Vavatsinia take the road north towards Machairas Monastery. Kionia picnic site is located in Machairas Forest about 8km from Vavatsinia village. From there, continue 1km north on the road towards Machairas to a picnic table with benches in a road bend. This is close to the starting point and there is space for parking.

This trail explores the Machairas Forest. Magnificent views towards the north accompany you as you walk steeply downhill on the often loose, stony path. From Mantra tou Kampiou climb the narrow paths described here and you will be spoilt with views of forested slopes.

From the picnic bench in a road bend follow the tarmac road downhill for 700m. Leave the tarmac road by the map board to the right via stone steps. As you start the steep descent on the loose path, you almost immediately have views to the surrounding mountains. Notice a clear path on the right (you will return to this junction from the path on the right) and continue straight on.

The path swings steadily downhill with fine views towards Nicosia and the Kyrenia range. As you look back, the peak of Kionia with its radar dome stands out from the pine-covered mountains. After a steep descent of about 15min the path levels out for a short while, and from the ridge you have more views. The main vegetation, as is typical of this area, is pine trees, golden oaks and rock roses.

Continue, often on steep and loose surfaces, for a further 30–40min with excellent views to the mountains and towards Nicosia. After a long descent, at the path junction with signs, keep left and arrive at a **stone hut** (at 880m) from where you can enjoy the panorama of the Mesaoria plains, the mountains and a network of dirt roads.

WALK 26 – KAKOKEFALOS – MANTRA TOU KAMPIOU TRAIL

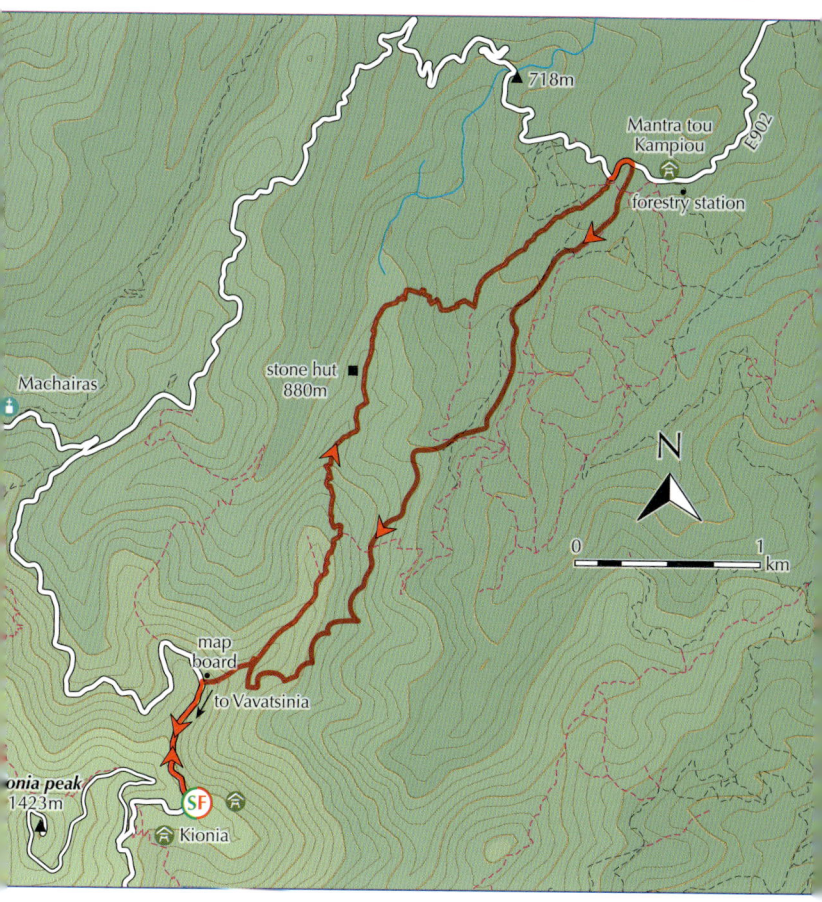

From the stone building, continue downhill and a few minutes later arrive at a junction. Ignore the wide track going uphill and keep right on the path as indicated by a walker sign. Zigzag downhill between pine trees for about 15min, and upon arriving at a dirt road, go left. The streambed of Mantra tou Kampiou snakes along on the right.

Ignore any adjoining tracks and about 15min later reach a tarmac road. Go right, and just before reaching the picnic site keep right on the unmarked dirt

Descend on the rocky path after passing the stone hut

track. (If you want to go to the **Mantra tou Kampiou picnic site** continue on the road. It is a large site with toilets, a water fountain, Machairas Forest information, a playground and plenty of picnic tables – a perfect place for a rest before the climb back to the start.)

The track crosses a fire break and then shortly after ignore a narrow path that crosses the track. About 600m from the tarmac road go right uphill on a clear path. Shortly after, when the path joins a fire break, stay on the left-hand side of the track and look out for a narrow path on the left. Take this narrow path that runs just below the ridge with a fire break. Crossing another fire break continue straight on with some far-reaching views on the left. Reach and cross a dirt track and continue straight on uphill on another fire break for about 30m. Go right on the narrow path fringed with rock roses that you follow on the mountainside for about 20min. When the path splits continue straight on and soon you can spot Kakokefalos viewpoint near the starting point.

Reach the path junction, go left and climb up to the tarmac lane, where keep left and follow it for 700m back to the starting point.

WALK 27
Dhyo Mouttes

Start/finish	Dhyo Mouttes trail head 1km south of Kionia picnic site (N34.91420, E33.19630)
Distance	4.5km
Total ascent/descent	225m
Grade	1
Time	1hr 30min
Refreshments	None along the trail
Access	From the A1 take the E105 road towards Vavatsinia. The information board for the Paylias-Dhyo Mouttes Nature Trail is located approximately 7km from Vavatsinia village on the right-hand side of the road. Parking place for a few cars by the map board.

This short, delightful nature trail climbs two peaks and will provide some of the finest views of the Machairas mountains. You can add this short trail to your day when you visit the Machairas Monastery.

Walk uphill on the stony path with views towards the snaking tarmac road by the foot of Kionia peak. A few minutes after starting the trail, the path splits; keep right and walk uphill and instantly you are greeted by great views of the surrounding mountains.

The peak of Kionia dominates the views along much of the trail

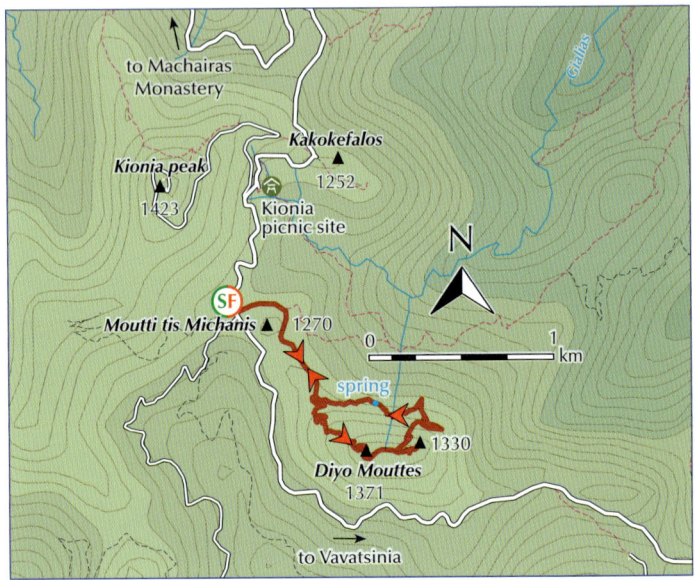

At the next junction – about 850m from the information board – bear right on wooden steps and then continue uphill between golden oaks. As you climb higher – about 30min from the start – you reach a viewpoint sign. A short, narrow path takes you to the first peak of Dhyo Mouttes (1371m) where you can enjoy an almost 360-degree panorama. Admire the views and retrace your steps back to the path and continue to the left.

Descending slightly, look for the salt lake near Limassol in the distance. Shortly reach another viewpoint on the second peak of Dhyo Mouttes (1356m) just off the path on the right. From here you can easily recognise Kionia peak, Nicosia, the Kyrenia range and the first viewpoint.

Retrace your steps to the path. As you descend, the Kionia peak is almost always visible. There are occasional steps as you zigzag downhill between golden oaks while continuing to enjoy excellent views towards Nicosia and the Kyrenia mountain range.

About 30min after the second viewpoint you arrive at Jeramias spring and shortly walk across deposits of talus rock and then pass by a site of a kiln. A few minutes after the spring you're back at the junction where you went uphill to the right; continue straight on and retrace your steps to the map board.

SOUTH AND EAST

Dramatic coastline near Pissouri (Walk 29)

Rolling hills near Kyparissia peak (Walk 30)

Larnaca and Limassol, with their busy taverns and restaurants, are the two largest towns on the coast. However, you might prefer to take in the stunning views from the quiet hill near the Germasogeia Dam, only a few kilometres from bustling Limassol.

The UNESCO-listed Kourion Archaeological Site is only 13km from Limassol; from the ruins of its ancient acropolis you can admire the magnificent views of Episkopi Bay. Agia Napa is well known for its tourist resorts and nightlife, and the beaches in the area are popular with sun-lovers, but at nearby Cape Greco you might spend a quiet evening hunting for fossils.

A spectacular trail follows the rugged coastline near Pissouri, and you can visit Petra tou Romiou where according to legend Aphrodite rose from the sea. Not too far from the busy coast lies the peaceful Hapotami river gorge with the abandoned village of Kato Archimandrita.

The coastal towns cater amply for tourists with a wide range of accommodation, and you can easily take day trips to Machairas Forest or Troodos.

WALK 28
Hapotami Trail

Start/finish	Kato Archimandrita church (N34.73673, E32.67993)
Distance	9.5km
Total ascent/descent	290m
Grade	1
Time	2hr 30min–3hr
Refreshments	None on route
Access	From Kouklia village take the F612 road towards Pano Archimandrita. Before reaching Pano Archimandrita leave the F612 to the right, signposted Kato Archimandrita. It is possible to park by the church opposite the only intact house in Kato Archimandrita.

Athough there are some well-kept plantations near the abandoned houses of Kato Archimandrita, it is a quiet place with a trickling stream meandering through the gorge. The often wide forest track follows the stream through the gorge and the water is crossed countless times. Leaving the stream behind, enjoy a bird's-eye view of the undisturbed sections of the deep gorge down below.

Kato Archimandrita, the lower part of the village of Archimandrita, was inhabited until 1962. However, its residents felt that the lack of school and suitable road to the upper part of the village isolated them, and they moved to Pano Archimandrita in 1962. Today the crumbling abandoned houses and an intact chapel dedicated to the Virgin Mary are what remains of the former village.

From the church, walk along the stony track between the ruins of houses to a building with an arched gate and with an **ancient olive tree** in its yard. Turn left by this building and walk alongside a fenced plantation to the stream.

Cross the stream(bed) for the first time and at the junction take the track on the right. As you walk beneath pine trees, wind turbines at the opposite side of the gorge soon come into view. The track follows the contour of the hillside and about 10-15min later reaches the stream again. Ignore a track on the right and continue straight on.

WALKING IN CYPRUS

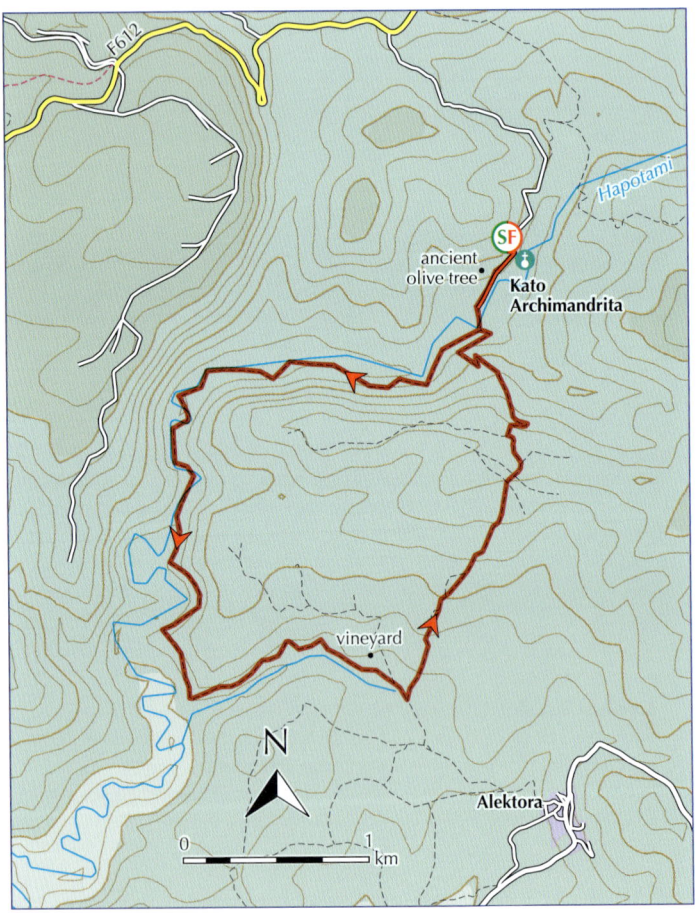

Over the next 20-25min you cross the stream numerous times on slippery rocks and often walk very close to it in the narrowing gorge. The track then bends slightly to the left and you start a gentle climb with the sight of the wind turbines on the top of the hills on the right. Walking by chalk walls, there is a mesmerising view to the surrounding hills and to the winding narrow gorge down below. Then as the track swings to the left there's a bird's-eye view of the narrow, dense gorge.

Soon pass a **vineyard** and then some olive trees on the right. Carry straight on, ignoring other paths, and shortly after the vineyard reach a grey gravel road. Turn left towards the hill. As you walk gently uphill by young olive trees, the houses of the distant village of Alektora can be seen on the right.

The grey gravel road changes into a stony track lined with shrubs and rock roses and then levels out a bit. About 20min after joining the grey gravel road, the track divides; keep right and a few minutes later at the junction bear left.

Carry straight on at the next junction; soon there are remarkable views down to the Hapotami river gorge and the ruined houses of Kato Archimandrita. Go downhill, and follow the winding track back to the junction and the stream where you first crossed. Retrace your steps back to the **church**.

The remains of Kato Archimandrita

WALK 29
Pissouri coast walk

Start/finish	Columbia Beach Resort, Pissouri (N34.64926, E32.71944)
Distance	Without the detour: 8.5km; with the detour to the pebble beach: 12.5km
Total ascent/descent	Without the detour: 260m; with the detour to the beach: 610m
Grade	2
Time	Without the detour: 3hr; with the detour to the pebble beach: 4hr 30min
Refreshments	In Pissouri village, but none along the way
Access	Pissouri Beach is located along the B6 road approximately halfway between Paphos and Limassol. From the B6 road turn off to F609 and follow it to Columbia Beach resort. There is a place to park close to the sea.

This circular route follows some marked trails with an option to make a detour to a hidden pebble beach. As you walk along an often crumbling narrow path along the coast you can enjoy some remarkable views to the rugged white limestone coastline. The turquoise sea crashes against the cliffs far below as you make your way along the trail. The second part of the route follows tracks with views to the sea.

Extra care should be taken on the cliffs as the surface can be very loose in places. There is no shade and it can get very hot on a sunny day. Take plenty of water and sun protection.

There are three different theories regarding the origin of the name **Pissouri**. The first is that it comes from the name of the ancient town of Voousoura. The second is that it derives from the Greek for 'very dark', as legend has it that the apostles met up in this area secretly at night. The third theory is that the name originates from the word *pissa* (resin), as that was the main product in this area during the Byzantine period. Today the scenic beach and the village on the hillside with its narrow streets attract many tourists.

Starting by the **Columbia Beach Resort**, walk towards the sea on a dirt track which bears slightly right. With the sea on your left, follow the wide path to the map

WALK 29 – PISSOURI COAST WALK

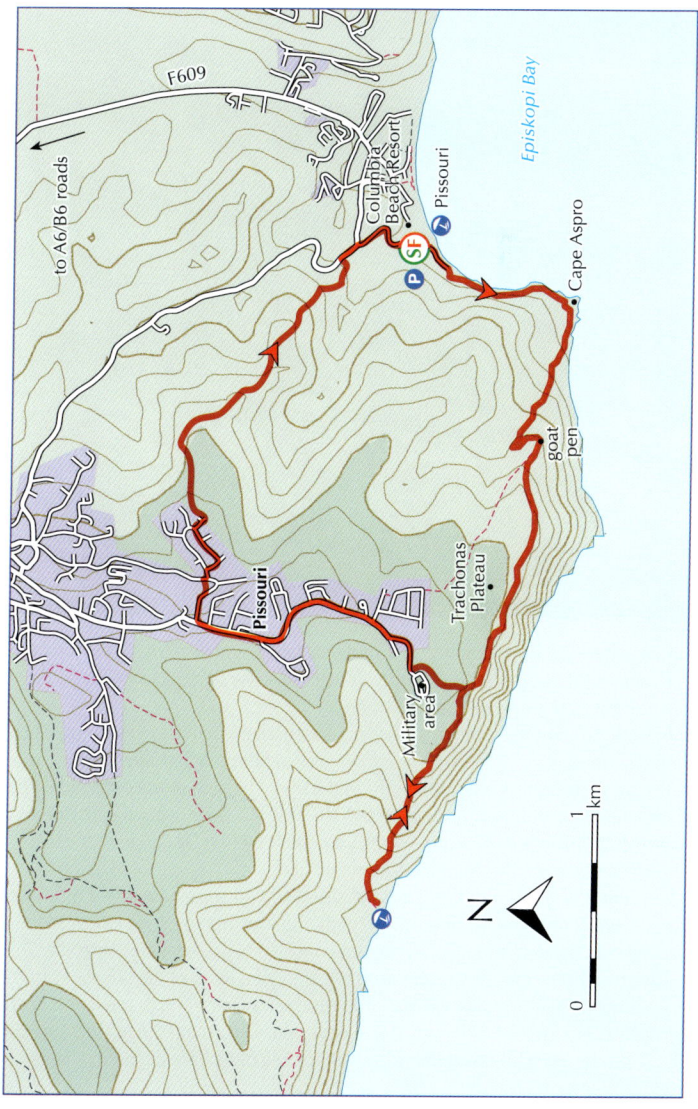

View of the shoreline from the ridge path

board, where the narrow, stony path starts on the edge of the cliff. This first part of the route is the local Blue Trail, and you will see some signs. Looking back, there are already great views of Pissouri Beach.

Walk on the often eroded cliff-edge, occasionally marked with cairns. Soon descend on a loose, slippery surface towards a pebble beach (**Cape Aspro**). Cross a dry streambed and continue uphill on the rocky hillside on its other side. The path turns slightly inland, away from the sea. This is a steep section with interesting rock formations to look out for, as you climb higher. The slope is constantly exposed to erosion, therefore the path might alter.

There is a gorge on the right-hand side and you soon pass a few old olive trees. Continue on the narrow, eroded path and look out for stone cairns as they are the only signs – although they are not consistently placed along the route. The undergrowth becomes denser as you curve along the ledge of the gorge.

About 30min into the walk (at around 2km), reach a rough track and keep left uphill, to reach an old, ramshackle **goat pen**. Go around the fenced area on the cliff-edge, then go up on the ridge with the sea on your left, ignoring the track just after the pen.

Huge, white chalky cliffs towering above the sea fill the horizon and after walking uphill on the ridge you reach the grassy **Trachonas Plateau**. Soon join a dirt track and follow it for about 130m. The scenery is interrupted by a military building with a radar and further in the distance by a telecommunications antenna.

Detour to the pebble beach

If you want to continue on the cliff top and descend to a pebble beach then when the track bends right towards the **military building**, leave it and stay close to the sea. The path runs along the edge and the wind turbines near the Hapotami gorge come into view.

As you walk along a ridge with views to the turquoise sea on the left and to a gorge and hills on the right, you'll soon see a long pebble beach. Shortly the path starts to descend. You can go all the way down to the beach but the ground is very loose and steep. You will also have to climb back along the very same path. There are cairns along the route but you might have to alter your way in some places.

The remote **beach** is a peaceful spot for a rest before retracing your steps to **Pissouri** or to the track near the military area.

Main route continued

Take the track towards the military building and soon you walk with the fence on your left. Reach a track by the entrance of the military area and keep right. Shortly after meet a tarmac lane by a villa and go right. Follow Kolokotroni Street among houses, ignoring any side roads. Go right on Panoramatos Street and as it bends left, keep right on Leforos Omirou road. Almost immediately go right on Odysseus Street and a few paces later turn left to Ektoros Street. Just before it bends left go right (Achaion Street) and the track starts on the left by the transformer building. This part of route is also known locally as the Red Trail. Follow this rough track downhill with some views towards the coast. It will lead down to a tarmac lane, go right and then take the first right and arrive back at the starting point.

WALK 30
Kyparissia Trail

Start/finish	Germasogeia Dam car park, about 700m from Foinikaria village centre (N34.75632, E33.09616)
Distance	12km
Total ascent/descent	630m
Grade	2
Time	4hr
Refreshments	None on the way: take plenty of drinking water
Access	From the direction of Limassol, take the F128 road and turn towards Foinikaria. Pass a viewpoint, turn left on the next road (Frakti Street) and follow this to Germasogeia Dam car park.

Very close to lively Limassol, these pleasant paths lead up to Kyparissia's peak where you can enjoy views towards Limassol on the coast and the nearby Germasogeia Dam. The first part of the trail climbs steadily uphill with views to pine tree-dotted slopes. The walk includes the main section of the Kyparissia Nature Trail. There is very little shade on the hillside so it can get very hot on sunny days.

From the car park, walk on the tarmac road uphill for about 700m and then turn left towards Calabria. Go for a further 300m, where a walker sign marks the start of the trail on the left. Follow the wide rocky track for about 10–15min with views towards the dam and Foinikaria village. Go left uphill on a dirt track as the walker sign indicates, and about 15min later leave it to the right when you see an arrow.

Follow the winding, stony path uphill with views of the surrounding hills. Ahead is a small sharp peak and the dam is slightly behind you at this point. The surrounding hillside is scattered with pine and olive trees. The path swings to the left and a steep towering hillside obstructs the view to the left for a few minutes. Shortly, the hill gives way to fine views again towards the dam and Limassol on the far left.

Soon spot a roofed viewing platform in front of you at the top of the hill, then reach a small **information board** with a map of the nature trail. Here the path splits; keep left. (You will return from the hill on the other path.) The narrow, stony path climbs steadily with great views to the dam, Limassol, the salt lake and the coastline. Here you will see the familiar nature trail labels naming some of the bushes and trees.

WALK 30 – KYPARISSIA TRAIL

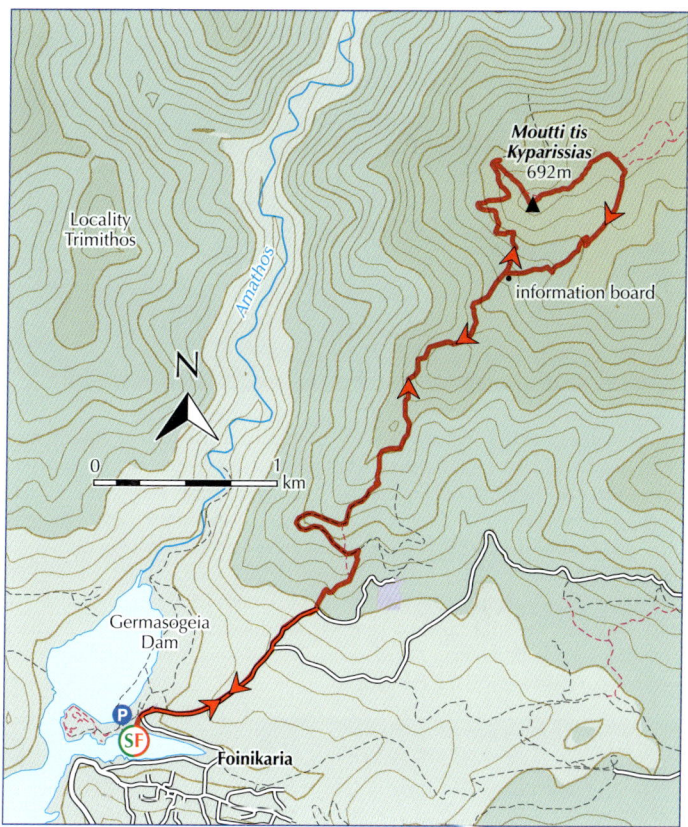

About 15min after the path split, reach a dirt track. Keep right and soon reach a sign: 'Kyparissia Peak 100m'. Turn right to make your final ascent to **Moutti tis Kyparissias** (692m).

On **Moutti tis Kyparissias** there is a roofed viewpoint that you may have seen earlier. Take a break on a bench and enjoy the excellent panorama towards Limassol and the coast. The mountain's name refers to the numerous cypress trees that populate it, especially on its higher sections.

The narrow path leads to the top of Moutti tis Kyparissias

Continue downhill on the wide track just behind the viewpoint. Shortly after, at an unmarked intersection, keep right and very soon reach another junction where you bear right, downhill. Shortly, at the next intersection, go right again as the green walker sign indicates. In front of you, between the crowns of trees, are views towards Limassol. As you descend, pines and junipers offer occasional shade.

About 30min after leaving Kyparissia's peak, reach and cross a bridge and then walk with the streambed on your left and a few minutes later arrive back at the junction with the **map board** where the path split. Continue straight and retrace your steps back to the **car park**.

Views towards Germasogeia dam and Limassol

WALK 31
Stavrovouni Monastery

Start/finish	Stavrovouni Monastery car park (N 34.887192 E33.436717)
Distance	5.5km
Total ascent/descent	345m
Grade	1
Time	2hr
Refreshments	None along the trail
Access	From the A1 high road or B1 road take F106 that leads to the monastery. Car park near the monastery.

While many drive up to the monastery to enjoy the extensive panorama, you can also follow this short trail that takes you below the monastery. The first and last section of the described trail is part of the long-distance E4 trail and far-reaching views accompany you during the entire route.

According to legend, Stavrovouni Monastery was founded by Saint Helen in the 4th century and therefore it is considered one of the oldest monasteries in the world, and the earliest documented on the island. The main relic in the Greek Orthodox monastery is a fragment of the Holy Cross. The monks live by very strict rules, and only men are allowed to visit the monastery.

The trail starts outside the gate near the All Saints church. The narrow path skirts behind the church building and almost immediately you can enjoy the excellent panorama towards the coast.

Descend on steps towards the big **cross** on the hillside. To enjoy further views you can make a short detour to the cross. The path bends right as you descend, and the monastery is perched like a fort on the hill above you. When the path splits head to the second cross. From there you continue descending with stunning views. Zigzag steeply downhill often on loose ground for about 10-15min and reach a track near a **farm**. Keep right slightly uphill and follow the track on the mountainside. At the track junction go right. The track swings on the mountainside with a gully on the left and the monastery building on the peak is almost always visible.

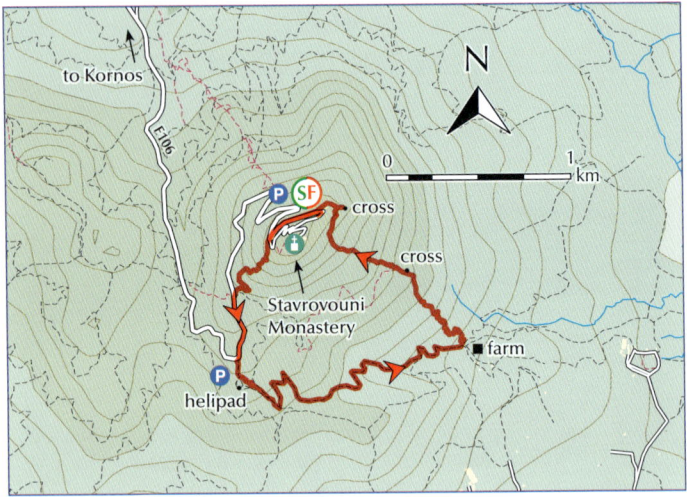

At the next junction take the path between tracks uphill. Zigzag up to reach a track, go right and arrive at a car park/picnic site by the road. Follow the road right uphill for a few mins and where the E4 path crosses the tarmac lane, go right uphill on the path that runs between the track and the tarmac lane. Climb with views towards the coast; you can also make out Kionia peak and the Kyrenia mountains in the far distance. Reach the tarmac lane again, go uphill and shortly after arrive back at the monastery.

Wooden cross at a viewpoint below Stavrovouni Monastery

Stavrovouni Monastery

WALK 32
Kavos Hill and sea caves

Start/finish	Cavo Greco Visitor Centre (N34.970400, E34.070849)
Distance	6.5km
Total ascent/descent	150m
Grade	1
Time	2hr
Refreshments	Café at the Visitor Centre
Access	Arriving from the direction of Agia Napa on the E306, turn off onto the E307 towards Cavo Greco Visitor Centre. There is a car park opposite the Visitor Centre. Buses from Agia Napa.

Just a stone's throw from the busy beaches of Agia Napa lies Cape Greco National Park, a protected area and part of the Natura 2000 conservation project. The dramatic coastline washed by turquoise water is explored by boat by many holidaymakers. The trail described here is a popular one, and in particular the viewpoint on top of Kavos Hill is a favourite among visitors as it can be accessed from a nearby car park. From here you can enjoy the panorama of the rugged coast. Look out for fossils as you pass rocks along the trail.

From the car park opposite the Visitor Centre take the path signed as 'Aphrodite Nature Trail' and head towards the sea. Follow the well-trodden path and shortly pass a site of an ancient temple. At the path junction go right signposted to Sea Caves. Head towards the National Guard Camp and Kavos Hill. Shortly after at the next junction keep left below the military area. Reach a track near the sea and turn right. Follow this wide path with towering rocks on your right and the sea on your left. There is a network of paths; stay on the well-trodden path closer to the rocks and soon your path merges with the E4 trail.

Keep an eye out for a path that goes uphill on the right. Ascend on this narrow stony path and when it splits keep right. There are some faint trails on the hillside but stay on the well-trodden path snaking uphill, with views to the sea. Reach a dirt road, keep left and shortly arrive at a roofed viewpoint on top of Kavos Hill. The rugged coastline leads the eye all the way to Agia Napa.

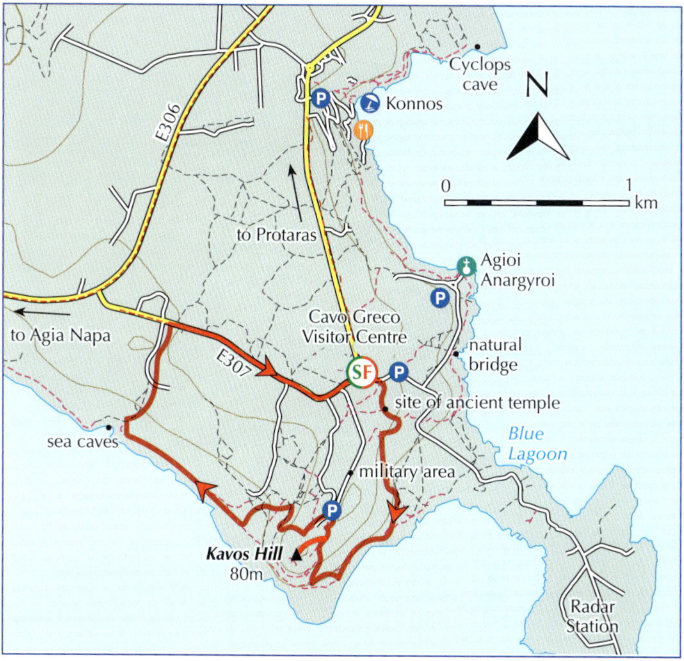

WALK 32 – KAVOS HILL AND SEA CAVES

Path leading through rocky landscape

Extensive views from Kavos Hill

Drink in the view and then go downhill on the dirt track that leads to a car park. Go left on the track that soon becomes a path as you head towards the sea. As you descend the path curves right and brings you down to a wide path with signs; go right (this is signed as the Sea Caves Nature Trail). Shortly after at the junction go left towards the sea caves. There are several paths; head diagonally towards the sea to meet a well-trodden path closer to the rugged shore and continue with the sea on your left. Some 10-15min from the last signposted junction, reach the sea caves.

From the sea caves head to the car park and continue on the track to reach the E307 road with a bike lane. Turn right and follow the bike lane back to the Visitor Centre which is about 1km away.

AGIA NAPA SEA MONSTER

Legend has it that a sea monster lives in the waters of Agia Napa. Fishermen call it *To Filiko Teras* (The Friendly Monster) as it never harmed humans, but was known to drag away fishing nets. Many believe that the sea monster is connected to Scylla, the sea creature from Greek mythology that appears on mosaics in the House of Dionysos in Paphos. Many tourists board boats in the hope of getting a glimpse of the legendary sea creature.

As you walk along the coastal paths of Capo Greco, you are more likely to see fossils of former creatures than the legendary sea monster.

WALK 33
Agioi Anargyroi – Cyclops Cave

Start/finish	Cavo Greco Visitor Centre (N34.970400, E34.070849)
Distance	6.5km
Total ascent/descent	110m
Grade	1
Time	2hr
Refreshments	Café at the visitor centre, and café and restaurant at Konnos/Konnoi Beach
Access	Arriving from the direction of Agia Napa on the E306, turn right onto the E307 towards Cavo Greco Visitor Centre. There is a car park opposite the visitor centre.

Follow the rugged coastline first to the symbolic rock arch and then to a chapel. As you continue to Konnos Beach there are amazing views of lazily rocking boats on the turquoise sea. There is no shade on this trail so it can get really hot between May and October, but you can stop for a swim at Konnos Beach before you continue to the Cyclops cave.

Agioi Anargyroi church

WALKING IN CYPRUS

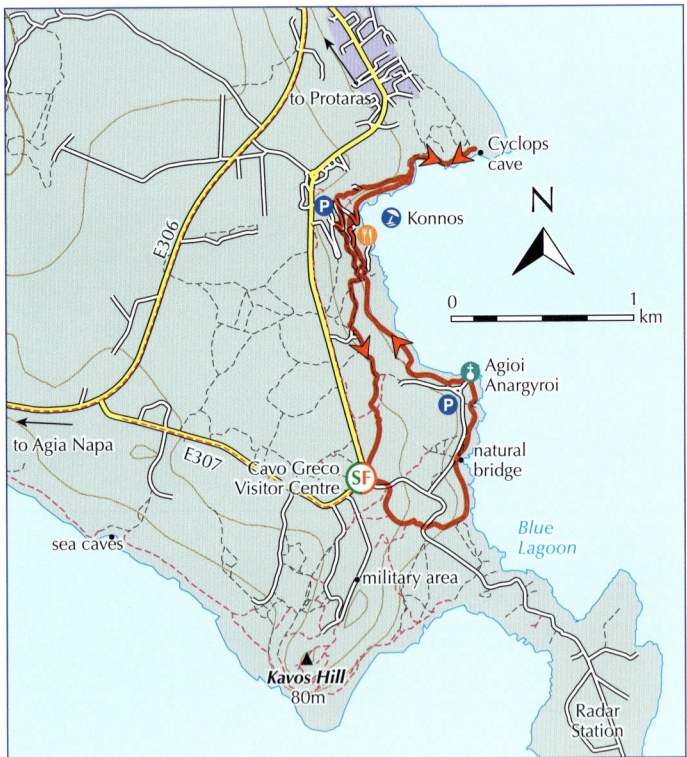

From the parking area opposite the visitor centre, take the path signed as 'Aphrodite Nature Trail'. Follow this well-trodden path towards the sea, passing a site of an ancient temple. There are some views towards the nearby Kavos Hill. At the path junction with signs go left towards Agioi Anargyroi. Ignore any other paths and stay on the wide path. Cross a tarmac road and continue on its other side, shortly meeting a path near the sea and keeping left. At 1km pass Kamara tou Koraka (**rock bridge**) and continue with the sea on your right to Agioi Anargyroi Chapel. From the church follow the Agioi Anargyroi path, with the sea on your right, towards Konnos Beach, which is visible from the church. At the big path junction keep right and shortly after reach a track, then go right downhill.

WALK 33 – AGIOI ANARGYROI – CYCLOPS CAVE

There are other paths in the bush but always keep close to the sea if there isn't an E4 sign or an arrow to indicate direction.

Walk towards the beach and the hotel building on the slope. A few steps lead downhill; arrive at a path, go right as an arrow indicates and then the path swings to the left by the sea. About 30min after leaving the church, arrive at **Konnos Beach**.

Walk across the beach, climb up to the barren slope and continue with the sea on your right. When the path splits, keep right downhill, closer to the sea (the other path goes the same way but on the upper level). When the path splits again keep right, closer to the sea. The path might be a bit eroded in places so take care. Soon you will arrive at a rocky clearing where there is a viewpoint and steps leading down to the **cave**.

After visiting the cave, climb up to an area that is used for parking and head towards the row of modern houses. Take the path after the houses with the sea on your left. Follow this upper path towards Konnos Beach. When the path splits keep right and ignore the path on the left that leads down to the beach, and the

Cyclops cave

steps on the right leading to a hotel. Stay on the path that takes you to Konnos Beach car park. Follow the tarmac lane and take the path on the left as the lane bends right. Ignore a path on the left and at the junction go right turning slightly away from the sea. At the rough path junction go left and shortly after take the path on the right by the fire hydrant N6. At the next junction continue straight on, and on reaching a stony path keep right towards Kavos Hill. Meet the bike lane, go left and arrive back at the visitor centre.

CYCLOPS

Cyclops is a giant, one-eyed, strong and wild creature of Greek mythology. The word *cyclops* means 'round- or circle-eyed'.

In Homer's *Odyssey*, when Odysseus arrived on the Island of Cyclops he found a cave and he and his men ate the food that was inside it. But the cave was home to Polyphemus, who was a cyclops. The cyclops returned to his cave in the evening and trapped Odysseus and his crew and ate some of the men. Odysseus hatched an escape plan: he gave Polyphemus some strong wine and then blinded him. When the cyclops, groaning in pain, asked who had attacked him, Odysseus told him: nobody. In the morning, as Polyphemus was letting his sheep out, he touched each animal's back to check if anyone was riding on them, but the men left the cave tied to the bellies of the sheep.

According to cyclops stories, the creature had a link with blacksmithing, since blacksmiths covered one eye with an eye patch so that flying sparks wouldn't blind them in both eyes.

Another possible explanation of the cyclops legend was uncovered in 1914, when prehistoric dwarf elephant skulls were found on Cyprus, Crete, Malta and Sicily. The paleontologist Othenio Abel suggested that the central cavity in the skull might have been a large single eye socket.

APPENDIX A
Useful contacts

Tourist information

Cyprus Tourism Organisation
www.visitcyprus.com

Official site of Troodos mountains
www.mytroodos.com

Troodos Visitor Centre
tel +357 2542 0144

Paphos/Baf information
www.visitpafos.org.cy
www.choosecyprus.com
www.limassoltourism.com
www.visitnicosia.com.cy

Tourist information offices

Southern Cyprus
Nicosia/Lefkosia
tel +357 2267 4264

Limassol
tel +357 2532 3211

Platres
tel +357 2542 1316

Larnaca
tel +357 2465 4322

Paphos/Baf
tel +357 2693 2841

Agia Napa
tel +357 2372 1796

Polis
tel +357 2632 2468

Transport

Airports
Larnaca International Airport
www.hermesairports.com

Paphos International Airport
www.hermesairports.com

Flight operators (from UK)
Easyjet
www.easyjet.com

Ryanair
www.ryanair.com

British Airways
www.britishairways.com

Jet2
www.jet2.com

Thomas Cook
www.thomascook.com

Local bus operators
Intercity Buses
www.intercity-buses.com

Pafos Buses
www.pafosbuses.com

Cyprus By Bus
www.cyprusbybus.com

Limassol Airport Express
www.limassolairportexpress.eu

Limassol Buses
www.limassolbuses.com

Car rental

In Cyprus you will find the well-known international car rental companies, as well as local car hire companies. Details can be found online using an internet search engine.

Accommodation

Cyprus listings
www.cyprus.com

Bookcyprus.com
www.bookcyprus.com

Booking.com
www.booking.com

Trivago
www.trivago.co.uk

Expedia
www.expedia.co.uk

Emergencies

European emergency number: 112

Forest Fire: 1407

APPENDIX B
Further reading

Books

Lawrence Durrell, *Bitter Lemons of Cyprus*, Faber & Faber, 1951

Victoria Hislop, *The Sunrise*, Headline Review, 2015

Stella Kalogeraki, *Greek Mythology*, Mediterraneo Editions, 2004

Gregory S Lamb, *The People In Between: Cyprus Odyssey*, CreateSpace, 2012

John McPhee, *Annals of the Former World*, Farrar, Straus and Giroux, 1998

George Sfikas, *Wild Flowers of Cyprus*, Efstathiadis Group, 1992

Colin Thubron, *Journey into Cyprus*, Vintage, 2012

Websites

www.greekmythology.com (Greek mythology)

www.ancient.eu/cyprus (ancient history)

www.cypruswildflowers.com (nature)

www.aboutcyprus.org.cy (history, nature, culture)

DOWNLOAD THE GPX FILES

All the routes in this guide are available for download from:

www.cicerone.co.uk/1290/GPX

as standard format GPX files. You should be able to load them into most online GPX systems and mobile devices, whether GPS or smartphone. You may need to convert the file into your preferred format using a conversion programme such as gpsvisualizer.com or one of the many other such websites and programmes.

When you follow this link, you will be asked for your email address and where you purchased the guidebook, and have the option to subscribe to the Cicerone e-newsletter.

www.cicerone.co.uk

LISTING OF CICERONE GUIDES

BRITISH ISLES CHALLENGES, COLLECTIONS AND ACTIVITIES

Great Walks on the England Coast Path
Map and Compass
The Big Rounds
The Book of the Bivvy
The Book of the Bothy
The Mountains of England and Wales
   Vol 1 — Wales
   Vol 2 — England
The National Trails
Walking the End to End Trail
Cycling Land's End to John o' Groats

LAKE DISTRICT

Bikepacking in the Lake District
Cycling in the Lake District
Joss Naylor's Lakes, Meres and Waters of the Lake District
Lake District Winter Climbs
Lake District: High Level and Fell Walks
Lake District: Low Level and Lake Walks
Mountain Biking in the Lake District
Outdoor Adventures with Children — Lake District
Scrambles in the Lake District — North
Scrambles in the Lake District — South
Trail and Fell Running in the Lake District
Walking The Cumbria Way
Walking the Lake District Fells
   — Borrowdale
   — Buttermere
   — Coniston
   — Keswick
   — Langdale
   — Mardale and the Far East
   — Patterdale
   — Wasdale
Walking the Tour of the Lake District

NORTH-WEST ENGLAND AND THE ISLE OF MAN

Walking the King Charles III England Coast Path: North West
Walking the King Charles III England Coast Path: North West
   — Cumbria Map Booklet
   — Lancashire and Merseyside Map Booklet
Cycling the Pennine Bridleway
Walking the Pennine Way
Walking the Pennine Way Map Booklet
Isle of Man Coastal Path
The Lune Valley and Howgills
Walking in Cumbria's Eden Valley
Walking in Lancashire
Walking in the Forest of Bowland and Pendle
Walking on the Isle of Man
Walking on the West Pennine Moors
Walking the Ribble Way
Hadrian's Wall Path

Hadrian's Wall Path Map Booklet
The Coast to Coast Cycle Route
The Coast to Coast Map Booklet
The Coast to Coast Walk

NORTH-EAST ENGLAND, YORKSHIRE DALES AND PENNINES

Walking the Dales Way
The Dales Way Map Booklet
Cycling the Reivers Route
Cycling the Way of the Roses
Cycling in the Yorkshire Dales
Great Mountain Days in the Pennines
Mountain Biking in the Yorkshire Dales
The Cleveland Way and the Yorkshire Wolds Way
The Cleveland Way Map Booklet
The North York Moors
Trail and Fell Running in the Yorkshire Dales
Walking in County Durham
Walking in Northumberland
Walking in Northumberland
Walking in the North Pennines
Walking in the Yorkshire Dales
   — North and East
   — South and West
Walking St Cuthbert's Way
Walking St Oswald's Way and Northumberland Coast Path

DERBYSHIRE, PEAK DISTRICT AND MIDLANDS

Cycling in the Peak District
Dark Peak Walks
Scrambles in the Dark Peak
Walking in Derbyshire
Walking in the Peak District
   — White Peak East
   — White Peak West

SOUTHERN ENGLAND

20 Classic Sportive Rides in South East England
20 Classic Sportive Rides in South West England
Bikepacking — South East Gravel
Cycling in the Cotswolds
Mountain Biking on the North Downs
South West Coast Path Map Booklet
   — Vol 1: Minehead to St Ives
   — Vol 2: St Ives to Plymouth
   — Vol 3: Plymouth to Poole
Suffolk Coast and Heath Walks
The Cotswold Way
The Cotswold Way Map Booklet
The Kennet and Avon Canal
The Lea Valley Walk
The Lea Valley Walk
The North Downs Way
North Downs Way Map Booklet
The Peddars Way and Norfolk Coast Path

The Pilgrims' Way
The Ridgeway National Trail
The Ridgeway Map Booklet
The South Downs Way
The South Downs Way Map Booklet
The Thames Path
The Thames Path Map Booklet
The Two Moors Way
Two Moors Way Map Booklet
Walking Hampshire's Test Way
Walking in Essex
Walking in Kent
Walking in London
Walking in Norfolk
Walking in the Chilterns
Walking in the Cotswolds
Walking in the Isles of Scilly
Walking in the New Forest
Walking in the North Wessex Downs
Walking on Dartmoor
Walking on Guernsey
Walking on Jersey
Walking on the Isle of Wight
Walking the Dartmoor Way
Walking the Jurassic Coast
Walking the Sarsen Way
Walking the South West Coast Path
Walks in the South Downs National Park

WALES AND WELSH BORDERS

Cycle Touring in Wales
Cycling Lon Las Cymru
Great Mountain Days in Snowdonia
Hillwalking in Shropshire
Mountain Walking in Snowdonia
Offa's Dyke Path
Offa's Dyke Map Booklet
Scrambles in Snowdonia
Snowdonia: 30 Low-level and Easy Walks
   — North
   — South
The Cambrian Way
The Pembrokeshire Coast Path
Pembrokeshire Coast Path Map Booklet
The Snowdonia Way
The Wye Valley Walk
Walking Glyndwr's Way
Walking in Carmarthenshire
Walking in Gower
Walking in Pembrokeshire
Walking in the Brecon Beacons
Walking on Gower
Walking the Severn Way
Walking the Shropshire Way
Walking the Wales Coast Path

SHORT WALKS SERIES

15 Short Walks in Dumfries and Galloway
15 Short Walks in Perthshire North — Pitlochry, Aberfeldy and Dunkeld
15 Short Walks in the Scottish Borders
15 Short Walks in the Trossachs —

Callander and Aberfoyle
15 Short Walks on the Isle of Mull
15 Short Walks on the Isle of Skye
15 Short Walks on the Orkney Islands
15 Short Walks on the Shetland Islands
15 Short Walks Hadrian's Wall
15 Short Walks in the Lake District
— Keswick, Borrowdale and Buttermere
— Windermere Ambleside and Grasmere
— Coniston and Langdale
15 Short Walks in Arnside and Silverdale
15 Short Walks in the Ribble Valley
15 Short Walks in Nidderdale
15 Short Walks in Northumberland — Wooler, Rothbury, Alnwick and the coast
15 Short Walks in the Yorkshire Dales
— Grassington, Skipton, Malham and Ilkley
— Sedbergh, Kirkby Lonsdale and Ingleton
15 Short Walks in the Peak District — Bakewell and the White Peak
15 Short Walks in the Peak District — Edale and the Hope Valley
15 Short Walks on the Malvern Hills
15 Short Walks Cheddar and the Mendips
15 Short Walks in Cornwall
— Newquay and the North Coast
— Falmouth and the Lizard
— Land's End and Penzance
15 Short Walks in Norfolk — Broads and Coast
15 Short Walks in South Devon — Salcombe, Brixham and the coast
15 Short Walks in the South Downs — Brighton, Eastbourne and Arundel
15 Short Walks in the Surrey Hills
15 Short Walks on Dartmoor North — Okehampton and Chagford
15 Short Walks on Dartmoor South — Ivybridge and Princetown
15 Short Walks on Exmoor
15 Short Walks on the Isle of Wight
15 Short Walks Winchester
15 Short Walks in Bannau Brycheiniog — Brecon Beacons
15 Short Walks in Pembrokeshire — Tenby and the south
15 Short Walks in the Forest of Dean

SCOTLAND

Ben Nevis and Glen Coe
Cycling in the Hebrides
Cycling in the Hebrides
Cycling the North Coast 500
Great Mountain Days in Scotland
Mountain Biking in Southern and Central Scotland
Mountain Biking in West and North West Scotland
Not the West Highland Way: A Mountain High Way
Scotland
Scotland's Best Small Mountains
Scottish Wild Country Backpacking
Skye Munros
Skye's Cuillin Ridge Traverse
The Borders Abbeys Way
The Hebridean Way
The Hebrides
The Isle of Skye
The Skye Trail
The Southern Upland Way
The West Highland Way
West Highland Way Map Booklet
Walking Ben Lawers, Rannoch and Atholl
Walking in the Cairngorms
Walking in the Pentland Hills
Walking in the Scottish Borders
Walking in the Southern Uplands
Walking in Torridon, Fisherfield, Fannichs and An Teallach
Walking Loch Lomond and the Trossachs
Walking on Arran
Walking on Harris and Lewis
Walking on Jura, Islay and Colonsay
Walking on Mull, Coll and Tiree
Walking on Rum and the Small Isles
Walking on the Orkney and Shetland Isles
Walking on Uist and Barra
Walking Rum and the Small Isles
Walking the Cape Wrath Trail
Walking the Corbetts
 Vol 1 — South of the Great Glen
 Vol 2 — North of the Great Glen
Walking the Fife Pilgrim Way
Walking the Galloway Hills
Walking the Great Glen Way
Walking the Great Glen Way Map Booklet
Walking the John o' Groats Trail
Walking the Munros
 Vol 1 — Southern, Central and Western Highlands
 Vol 2 — Northern Highlands and the Cairngorms
Winter Climbs in the Cairngorms
Winter Climbs: Ben Nevis and Glen Coe

ALPS CROSS-BORDER ROUTES

100 Hut Walks in the Alps
Alpine Ski Mountaineering Vol 1 — Western Alps
Hiking the Tour of Monte Rosa
The Karnischer Hohenweg
The Tour of the Bernina
Trail Running — Chamonix and the Mont Blanc region
Trekking Chamonix to Zermatt
Trekking in the Alps
Trekking in the Silvretta and Ratikon Alps
Trekking Munich to Venice
Trekking the Tour du Mont Blanc
Tour du Mont Blanc Map Booklet
Walking in the Alps

FRANCE, BELGIUM AND LUXEMBOURG

Camino de Santiago — Via Podiensis
Chamonix Mountain Adventures
Cycling London to Paris
Cycling the Canal de la Garonne
Cycling the Canal du Midi
Mont Blanc Walks
Mountain Adventures in the Maurienne
Short Treks on Corsica
The GR5 Trail — Through the French Alps
The GR5 Trail — Vosges and Jura
The Moselle Cycle Route
Trekking in the Vanoise
Trekking the Cathar Way
Trekking the GR10
Trekking the GR20 Corsica
Trekking the Robert Louis Stevenson Trail
Via Ferratas of the French Alps
Walking in Provence — East
Walking in Provence — West
Walking in the Auvergne
Walking in the Briannconnais
Walking in the Dordogne
Walking in the Haute Savoie: North
Walking in the Haute Savoie: South
Walking on Corsica
Walking the Brittany Coast Path
The GR5 Trail — Benelux and Lorraine
Walking in the Ardennes
The River Loire Cycle Route
The River Rhone Cycle Route
Cycling the Route des Grandes Alpes

PYRENEES AND FRANCE/SPAIN CROSS-BORDER ROUTES

Shorter Treks in the Pyrenees
The Pyrenean Haute Route
The Pyrenees
Trekking the Cami dels Bons Homes
Trekking the GR11 Trail
Walks and Climbs in the Pyrenees

SPAIN AND PORTUGAL

Camino de Santiago: Camino Frances
Coastal Walks in Andalucia
Costa Blanca Mountain Adventures
Cycling the Camino de Santiago
Mountain Walking in Mallorca
Mountain Walking in Southern Catalunya
Spain's Sendero Historico: The GR1
The Andalucian Coast to Coast Walk
The Camino del Norte and Camino Primitivo
The Camino Ingles and Ruta do Mar
The Mountains Around Nerja
The Mountains of Ronda and Grazalema
The Sierras of Extremadura
Trekking in Mallorca
Trekking in the Canary Islands
Trekking the GR7 in Andalucia
Walking and Trekking in the Sierra Nevada
Walking in Andalucia
Walking in Catalunya — Barcelona
Walking in Catalunya — Girona Pyrenees
Walking in the Picos de Europa
Walking La Via de la Plata and Camino Sanabres
Walking on Gran Canaria

Walking on La Gomera and El Hierro
Walking on La Palma
Walking on Lanzarote and Fuerteventura
Walking on Tenerife
Walking on the Costa Blanca
Walking the Camino dos Faros
Portugal's Rota Vicentina
The Camino Portugues
Walking in Portugal
Walking in the Algarve
Walking in the Algarve
Walking on Madeira
Walking on the Azores
Cycling the Ruta Via de la Plata

SWITZERLAND
Switzerland's Jura Crest Trail
The Swiss Alps
Tour of the Jungfrau Region
Trekking the Swiss Via Alpina
Walking in Arolla and Zinal
Walking in the Bernese Oberland — Jungfrau Region
Walking in the Engadine — Switzerland
Walking in Ticino
Walking in Zermatt and Saas-Fee

GERMANY
Hiking and Cycling in the Black Forest
The Danube Cycleway Vol 1
The Rhine Cycle Route
The Westweg
Walking in the Bavarian Alps
The Elbe Cycle Route

POLAND, SLOVAKIA, ROMANIA, HUNGARY AND BULGARIA
The Danube Cycleway Vol 2
The High Tatras
The Mountains of Romania

SCANDINAVIA, ICELAND AND GREENLAND
Hiking in Norway
 — North
 — South
Trekking the Kungsleden
Trekking in Greenland – The Arctic Circle Trail
Walking and Trekking in Iceland

SLOVENIA, CROATIA, SERBIA, MONTENEGRO AND ALBANIA
Hiking Slovenia's Juliana Trail
Mountain Biking in Slovenia
The Islands of Croatia
The Julian Alps of Slovenia
The Mountains of Montenegro
The Peaks of the Balkans Trail
The Slovene Mountain Trail
Walking in Slovenia: The Karavanke
Walking the Julian Alps of Slovenia
Walks and Treks in Croatia

ITALY
Alta Via 1 — Trekking in the Dolomites
Alta Via 2 — Trekking in the Dolomites
Day Walks in the Dolomites
Italy's Grande Traversata delle Alpi
Ski Touring and Snowshoeing in the Dolomites
The Way of St Francis: Via di Francesco
Trekking Gran Paradiso: Alta Via 2
Trekking in the Apennines
Trekking the Giants' Trail: Alta Via 1 through the Italian Pennine Alps
Via Ferratas of the Italian Dolomites
 — Vol 1
 — Vol 2
Walking Gran Paradiso National Park
Walking in Abruzzo
Walking in Italy's Cinque Terre
Walking in Italy's Stelvio National Park
Walking in Sicily
Walking in the Aosta Valley
Walking in the Dolomites
Walking in Tuscany
Walking in Umbria
Walking Lake Como and Maggiore
Walking Lake Garda and Iseo
Walking on the Amalfi Coast
Walking the Cammino Materano
Walking the Via Francigena Pilgrim Route
 — Part 1
 — Part 2
 — Part 3
 — Part 4
Walks and Treks in the Maritime Alps

IRELAND
The Wild Atlantic Way and Western Ireland
Walking the Kerry Way
Walking the Wicklow Way

INTERNATIONAL CHALLENGES, COLLECTIONS AND ACTIVITIES
Europe's High Points
Pocket First Aid and Wilderness Medicine

AUSTRIA
Innsbruck Mountain Adventures
Trekking Austria's Adlerweg
Trekking in Austria's Hohe Tauern
Trekking in Austria's Stubai Alps
Trekking in Austria's Zillertal Alps
Walking in Austria
Walking in the Salzkammergut: the Austrian Lake District

MEDITERRANEAN
Trekking in Greece
Walking and Trekking in Zagori
Walking and Trekking in Corfu
Walking on the Greek Islands — the Cyclades
Walking in Cyprus
Walking on Malta

HIMALAYA
8000 metres
Annapurna
Everest: A Trekker's Guide
Trekking in the Indian Himalayas
Trekking in the Karakoram

NORTH AMERICA
Hiking and Cycling the California Missions Trail
Hiking the Pacific Crest Trail
The John Muir Trail

SOUTH AMERICA
Aconcagua and the Southern Andes
Hiking and Biking Peru's Inca Trails
Trekking in Torres del Paine

AFRICA
Climbing Toubkal
Kilimanjaro
Walking in the Drakensberg
Walks and Scrambles in the Moroccan Anti-Atlas

NEW ZEALAND AND AUSTRALIA
Hiking the Overland Track

CHINA, JAPAN AND ASIA
Hiking and Trekking in the Japan Alps and Mount Fuji
Hiking in Hong Kong
Japan's Kumano Kodo Pilgrimage
Trekking in Bhutan
Trekking in Ladakh
Trekking in Tajikistan
Trekking in the Himalaya

TECHNIQUES
Fastpacking
The Mountain Hut Book

MINI GUIDES
Alpine Flowers
Navigation

MOUNTAIN LITERATURE
A Walk in the Clouds
Abode of the Gods
Fifty Years of Adventure
The Pennine Way – the Path, the People, the Journey
Unjustifiable Risk?

For full information on all our guides, books and eBooks,
visit our website:
www.cicerone.co.uk

CICERONE

Trust Cicerone to guide your next adventure, wherever it may be around the world...

Discover guides for hiking, mountain walking, backpacking, trekking, trail running, cycling and mountain biking, ski touring, climbing and scrambling in Britain, Europe and worldwide.

Connect with Cicerone online and find inspiration.

- buy books and ebooks
- articles, advice and trip reports
- GPX files and updates
- regular newsletter

cicerone.co.uk